The Corporate Executive's Guide
to General Investing

The Corporate Executive's Guide to General Investing

Paul Mladjenovic

BEP

BUSINESS EXPERT PRESS

Leader in applied, concise business books

The Corporate Executive's Guide to General Investing

Copyright © Business Expert Press, LLC, 2022.

Cover design by Charlene Kronstedt

Interior design by Exeter Premedia Services Private Ltd., Chennai, India

First published in 2022 by
Business Expert Press, LLC
222 East 46th Street, New York, NY 10017
www.businessexpertpress.com

ISBN-13: 978-1-63742-196-3 (paperback)
ISBN-13: 978-1-63742-197-0 (e-book)

Business Expert Press Finance and Financial Management Collection

First edition: 2022

10 9 8 7 6 5 4 3 2 1

Description

Successful corporate executives face unique investing challenges, because their personal wealth is irrevocably tied to their company's performance, normal market ups and downs, and even unexpected events. An executive's investment portfolio may consist mostly of employer stock and stock options that are governed by rules the executive doesn't know about and can't control. And the executive also faces a variety of other financial landmines, ranging from taxes to corporate pension shortfalls.

So the forward-thinking corporate executive badly needs effective financial management and investing strategies to build a financially secure future, designed with the special needs of a corporate executive in mind. That is what this guide will provide: the essence of what investments and investing strategies the executive should consider employing to achieve financial independence sooner, rather than later.

The audience for this investing guide includes C-suite executives, middle managers, and those in supervisory positions with executive responsibilities or aspirations. It will also be useful for MBA students, those in executive education seminars, and others who are planning corporate careers.

This book will teach the executive reader:

- How to set the proper goals before investing
- How to maximize corporate resources for your investing goals
- How to understand and choose from the different types of investments, including bank investments, stocks, mutual funds, exchange-traded funds (ETFs), venture capital investments, real estate investments, and alternative investments
- How to design an effective portfolio strategy for an executive's situation

The author Paul Mladjenovic was a CFP for 36 years and has extensive experience as a financial planner, educator, speaker, and author of the best-selling *Stock Investing for Dummies* and many other books in the fields of investing, finance, and entrepreneurship.

Keywords

investing; investing strategies; stocks; mutual funds; exchange-traded funds; ETFs; real estate; bonds; debt; executive; financial planning; financial independence

Contents

Introduction

Hello, my name is Paul Mladjenovic. And I'm an author of many books including the best-seller *Stock Investing for Dummies*, along with *High-Level Investing for Dummies, Investing in Gold and Silver for Dummies*, and *Zero-Cost Marketing*. And it has been a joy to write this particular book for you. In this, we're talking about you going from where you are an executive, corporate, or otherwise, and heading to the point where you are financially independent using general investing strategies. I've covered all the main aspects in this book, but let me tell you where they're at and how it's laid out.

First of all, the chapters are based on two basic phases, and that's to grow your money and then generating income once retirement is near. Growing your money means that your money is working as hard as you are during your career as a corporate executive.

Chapter 1 involves assumptions about investing and about you. This chapter also covers your financial starting point and your "target amount" that you need to reach with your investment assets to achieve financial independence. It is a simple dynamic that I refer to as the "crash course in retirement planning."

Chapter 2 highlights executive compensation since that will be the ultimate source of your funds and the foundation for your wealth-building program.

Chapters 3 to 7 focus on growth-related investments. The subject matter includes stocks, ETFs, mutual funds, real estate investing (REITs), and alternative investments. Keep in mind that some of these vehicles also do double-duty with excellent income potential.

For a focus on income strategies, head over to Chapters 8 (bonds) and 9 (retirement income strategies). If you have done even modestly growing your investments during your working years, converting them to a focus on income gives you the potential for a financially sound retirement.

Chapter 3 focuses on growth stocks. These will be crucial during your working years and you will learn the most important considerations for choosing wisely. You can switch to income-oriented stocks (dividend stocks) as you near your retirement years and this topic is more fully covered in Chapter 9.

I think that ETFs are an excellent and convenient vehicle for your portfolio. Same premise here ... choose growth-oriented ETFs (Chapter 4) during your working years and income-oriented ETFs during your retirement years (see Chapter 9).

Chapter 5 is on mutual funds, which are typically the foundation for most long-term retirement plans (401k plans, etc.) and other types of vehicles.

Then we'll get to real estate investing through one of my favorite vehicles in Chapter 6, which are real estate investment trusts (REITs). I think REITs are an excellent way to invest in a relatively easy, convenient, and hassle-free manner to include real estate in your portfolio.

Chapter 7 covers a few choice alternative investments. Gold, silver, and cryptocurrencies are covered as they are considered strong diversification versus traditional investment vehicles. I will also include bank investments here for short-term concerns.

Some important basic tax points and tax strategies are covered in Chapter 10. Understand wealth-building strategies versus taxes and how to minimize the taxes on your gains and income.

Each chapter will re-emphasize key points ("main takeaway points") and resources so you can dig deeper in that chapter's subject matter. And also about those vehicles you could take advantage of that'll help you build your wealth faster than ever before.

Lastly, since different investments tend to perform differently in various economic scenarios, it pays to monitor the "big picture" so you can optimize and customize your investing approach during ongoing macro events in the world of politics and the economy and financial markets so I have included an appendix listing these resources (blogs and websites) to keep you informed.

The bottom line is that you, as a corporate executive, have the power to flourish and attain prosperity and financial independence if you keep learning and working your investing action plan.

CHAPTER 1

Your Starting Point ... Plus Assumptions

Whether you are starting in your corporate executive position today as a junior, middle-level executive in a mid-sized firm or you are a C-level executive in a large, public firm, you can reach your financial objectives by maximizing the wealth you can accumulate through both your salary and your investment-related fringe benefits (such as stock options and 401k plan).

Your Action Plan Blueprint

The essence of building wealth during your career is a simple premise that has been tweaked and modified a thousand times by all sorts of advisers and financial consultants ... and here it is:

1. Inflow: Earn your money ... find ways to increase it.
2. Outflow: Spend less than you make ... find ways to decrease it.
3. Invest the difference. Repeat regularly until you reach your target amount for financial independence.
4. Maximize all your financial resources (greater income, 401k, etc.) to accelerate your journey to your target amount.

Yes ... the approach is simple ... but it's not easy. However, over a span of 20 to 40 years, very doable! Do this approach year in and year out and by the end of your working career it could be a seven-figure nest egg for a middle-class earner ... or an eight-figure sum for the industrious upper-income corporate executive.

You have heard it all before: "If you fail to plan ... then you plan to fail." The corporate job you have may give you some great perks now and some great income but to what extent will it be maximizing your career resources? Because the corporate executive is in a position to make an income that is significantly higher than the average worker, I think it's an important task for you to do the most simplest goal of all: coming up with the one number that if your assets grow to that point you will be financially self-sufficient or independent or at the point where you don't need to work that hard anymore.

From Focusing on Growth to Focusing on Income

Consider this an addendum to the overall action blueprint. It was about the "how" in terms of your overall approach, but this section accentuates the "what" involved in the approach. During your working years, the investments inside your various accounts should generally be focused on growth. Growth-oriented investments include

- Stocks (covered in Chapter 3)
- Exchange-traded funds (Chapter 4)
- Mutual funds (Chapter 5)
- Real estate (Chapter 6)
- Alternative assets (Chapter 7)

Later on and especially in your retirement years, the focus switches to income. Income-oriented investments include

- Bonds (covered in Chapter 8)
- Dividend stocks and other income strategies (Chapter 9)
- Real-estate income strategies (Chapter 6)

The Executive's Starting Point (Homework!)

Before you begin your journey to your financial independence target amount, like any journey, you need to know your starting point and the optimal path to your destination. Here is where your corporate skills will benefit you personally. It's time to create two important documents:

1. *Personal balance sheet.* What are your total assets, your total liabilities, and your net worth? The investable net worth is your starting point. This is what should be on the growth path to hit your retirement target.
2. *Personal cash flow statement.* From your total inflow (e.g., wages or net business income) less your outflow (expenses, debt payments, etc.) to figure out what you can comfortably invest as part of your accumulation and growth toward your personal target amount. Update this document regularly to know how much you can comfortably set aside for investing.

In terms of the amount(s) to invest, this includes what you can sock away not only in pretax, tax-advantaged accounts (401k, traditional IRAs, etc.) but also in after-tax vehicles (regular accounts, etc.). How much should you seek to invest? As much as possible. The real question is: How quickly do you want to reach a target amount that symbolizes your financial freedom?

The whole point of long-term investing is to build your wealth to the point where your wealth's potential cash flow (dividends, interest, etc.) makes work an option and not a necessity. Work is great ... but it should be something you enjoy and something that eventually becomes optional. The ultimate question when discussing your financial independence (such as a secure retirement) is that you woke up that morning and said to yourself: "What do I feel like doing today?" That is the essence of financial freedom in a single question. This is the essence of what I communicate in my retirement planning seminars and webinars. (For the reader's benefit, I include a link to a free retirement planning webinar in the resources listed at the end of this chapter.)

The Maximized 401k and Roth IRA Approach

Say you don't have a specific target amount for retirement, but you were specific in how much you plan to commit to your goal of financial freedom, how would that work out? Keep in mind that for higher-income folks, there may be limits to how much you can sock away so check with your tax adviser with your personal contribution limits. Regardless, I will assume relatively modest contributions for typical corporate compensation scenarios. Contributing a total of $20,000 in pretax accounts such as through some combination of a 401k plan and a Roth IRA, for example, is easily doable. If you did $20,000 per year for at least 30 years (averaging 10 percent total reinvested annual growth), how would you fare? If you were to plug in those numbers at financial websites that offer investment calculators (such as Bankrate.com and smartassets.com), that approach would accumulate over $3.6 million before factoring other variables such as tax rates and inflation, which can be hard to forecast decades in advance. The bottom line for you is that, in this example, $3.6 million, if invested in a portfolio of income securities yielding at least 3 percent, would earn you over $100,000 per year without touching the principal. But let's say that you will need $140,000 per year, how long would that $3.6 million last … again, presuming it is only yielding 3 percent?

In this case you would use an annuity calculator. Figure 1.1 is Bankrate's annuity calculator (found at www.bankrate.com/calculators/investing/annuity-calculator.aspx).

Plugging in your available numbers for our example and clicking on "Length of Annuity in years" gave the answer "46.76 years," which sounds comforting to me. Say you changed the yield from 3 percent to 3.5 percent … how long would your money last? In this case, that relatively modest increase of a half (0.5) percent extended the shelf life of that investment total to 59.21 years … nice!

Of course, you have the power to change the above for a more favorable result. What if, instead of socking away $20,000 annually for 30 years, it was 35 or 40 years? What if instead of $20,000 per year … you did $25,000 … or $30,000 … or more?

On the income side, what if you did better than 3 or 3.5 percent? How about 4 or 5 percent or better? What if you augmented your income strategy by writing call and put options which have the potential to increase the yield from your portfolio by an additional 3 or 5 or even 8 to 10 percent per year? What if you decreased your outflow (expenses and debt payments) by moving from a high-tax, high-cost state to a low-tax,

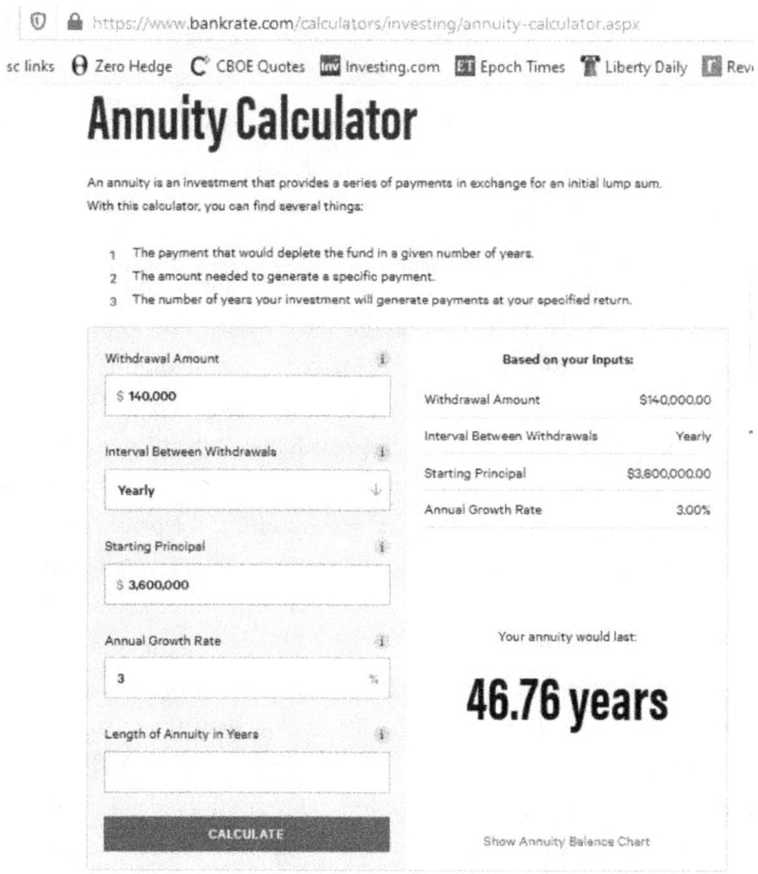

Figure 1.1 Bankrate calculator

low-cost state? Some of the best action ideas can start with "what if" questions.

I know one corporate executive that decided to maximize her 401k. She aggressively apportioned her salary so that the full 401k contribution allowable by law was immediately invested in the early part of the year to the point that her net pay (after all deductions including the 401k allotment) was less than $100! She wanted to reach the full 401k amount as early in the year as possible to take full advantage of time for the benefit of compounded growth. She could've spaced out the contribution more evenly throughout the year but she took very seriously the idea of time in her wealth-building approach. And yes ... she hit her target sooner than planned. So how badly do you want to hit your financial target(s)?

Crash Course Retirement Plan—The 5 to 10 Percent Assumption

Because we are planning for a future scenario, you can't avoid the fact that you must make assumptions. For my crash course on retirement planning, I do two assumptions: I assume 5 percent income potential (or yield) and I assume 10 percent growth. Why?

First off, both numbers are easy "back of the napkin" calculations for anyone and these ballpark assumptions are close enough, given market experiences going back decades. There have been stocks and ETFs I (or my students and clients) acquired years ago that had a dividend yield of 3 or 3.5 percent that today are yielding much higher than 5 percent. And the 10 percent growth? If you talk to a group of market analysts, you will hear that the market averaged annual growth of 8 to 11 percent in spite of what seems like a roller-coaster ride spanning decades. Additionally, successful long-term growth of 10 percent or better can be achieved not only based on what you invest in, but how. Dividend-paying stocks with dividend reinvestment plans (see Chapter 3 for details) and the investor's approach of "total reinvestment" can achieve the desired annual growth. In addition, most mutual funds (both growth oriented and income oriented) give you the ability to totally reinvest all dividends, interest, and capital gain distributions, which greatly enhance your annual growth above the nominal appreciation of merely own stocks and funds. And the "total reinvestment" approach is what anyone would do if they were serious about long-term wealth building.

The Four Retirement Scenarios and Your Response

Scenario A

Say, for example, that you expect to need $100,000 per year in retirement to have a comfortable retirement and, second, let's say that at the time of your retirement you're able to have a yield of 5 percent or greater from your asset. In this example, $100,000 per year at 5 percent per year backs up into a number of $2,000,000. This means that if you had $2,000,000 in financial assets and you put them into income-producing investments that gave you an average annual yield of at least 5 percent, you could

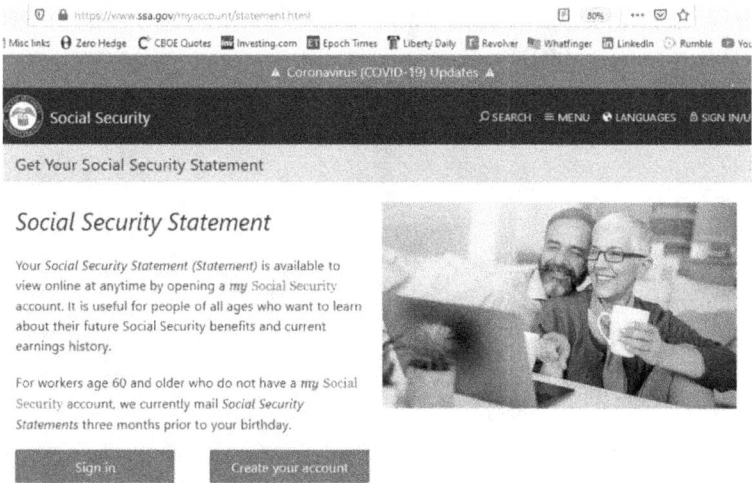

Figure 1.2 Social security

be able to achieve your $100,000 per annual income and able to reach a minimum level of financial independence without touching a penny of principal.

Scenario B

The income from your assets fell short? Then we go to plan B. This involves what your assets can do coupled with any pension and social security coming in (this is also referred to as "integration"). Let's cover social security since that is what virtually everyone is expecting. Make it a regular practice to check your social security earnings statement which also helps you estimate your future retirement benefits. Head over to their site at www.ssa.gov/myaccount (Figure 1.2).

This will help you learn about your benefits and help with your retirement planning.

Say that you learn from your social security statement that your projected earnings will be $25,000 per year starting in your first year. Now you know that the shortfall of $75,000 will be needed to be covered by cash flow from your investment portfolio.

Using 5 percent as the projected income yield, we now know that we don't need the full $2 million that we referenced as an example in the prior scenario. Since $75,000 is 5 percent of $1.5 million, our target amount is now $500,000 closer.

But let's say that you only have $1 million which implies a shortfall, what do you do next? Go to the next scenario.

Scenario C

Now we go to plan C which is about enhancing the return on your portfolio with either

- Getting higher income investment vehicles into your portfolio or
- Utilizing option writing to create income from your positions using either covered call options or selling put options. Either has the power to increase the annual cash flow from the portfolio by 3 to 8 percent and if it is done properly, it is relatively low risk.

A recent example is a client that had 200 shares of a high-priced stock going for $400 per share. She wrote a covered call on 100 shares of her stock and received premium (income) of $15,000. The terms of the option were that if the stock hit the agreed-upon price of $500 per share during the life of the option (it had nine months before it expired), then she would need to sell 100 shares at $500 per share. Now if the stock did not reach that price at any time during the nine-month duration of the call option, then the option would expire worthless, she would keep the premium income of $15,000, and she would also keep her stock.

A tutorial on covered call writing can be found with the options education site of the Options Industry Council at www.optionseducation. org/videolibrary/covered-calls.

Obviously go slow with this and learn about the strategy ... your financial adviser should be familiar with it. My clients and students learned to love the strategy as it can be a high-income and low-risk way to squeeze much more income from your stock and ETF portfolio. If your portfolio is $1 million and only earning $50,000 (a 5 percent yield) then it is not difficult to boost that to at least 8 percent using covered call option writing, meaning that the same portfolio can generate $80,000 in annual income easily covering the shortfall.

Scenario D

Plan D is the annuity structure approach. This means you would actually be cashing out some of the principal going forward and the ultimate issue is "Will the investment amount last as long (or longer) as your expected life span?" An example of this approach can be found earlier in this chapter but let's revisit it here.

You would take your asset total and put it into an annuity calculator. Enter your yield amount (say 3 percent) and then enter that you will draw down by $26,000 per year. If you only have $470,000, for example, then you can calculate for how long this total investment amount will last. Given that the $470,000 is being drawn down by $26,000 and only growing by 3 percent, it will last 25.29 years. If you are 65, then your assets would last until you reach age 90 (give or take a few months). That could be enough but the situation would likely require you to delay your retirement by a year or so or perhaps you could supplement your income with a part-time job or business.

Scenario E ... Active Wealth-Building Approach

The final approach ("plan E") means that you leave the realm of financial strategies and embrace active wealth-building strategies. When all investing and speculative strategies fall short, then you go to some combination of

- Lowering outflow. How can you lower your outflow? How can you decrease your expenses without too much pain? For some, it is leaving a high-tax state and moving to a low-tax state. According to recent state surveys, there could be as much as a 30 to 40 percent difference in living costs between a high-cost state and a low-cost state.
- Can you sell some dead or "nonearning" assets (such as collectibles or "stuff" in the basement, attic, or garage? I personally sold an item from my collectibles for $1,000.
- Job prospects. Can you continue working? Even another year or two can make a significant difference in the numbers.

- Can you start a part-time business? Many retirees have a wealth of knowledge and experience that can be converted into a fun and profitable business in their spare time.
- The Gig economy. Many folks are making some good money in their spare time by driving cars, consulting, designing web pages, or freelancing. Find out more at sites such as www.fiverr.com and www.upwork.com.

I'm always an advocate, where I tell everybody that they should have a part-time home business, because that adds another dimension to their wealth-building pursuits. And among the reasons why I tell them to do that is the obvious reason that a part-time home business will generate some extra supplemental income. The thing is, depending on how you structure it with your tax person's help, you might have the ability through that home business to be able to set up accounts that could really expand how much you're able to set aside for the future. You have accounts available for your home business such as Sep IRAs (resources in Chapter 10), for example, where you can be able to set aside up to $58,000 (the limit for 2021) per year as a percentage (25 percent as of 2021) of your net business income. And that means you can really sock away a tremendous amount for retirement.

In the meanwhile (until you retire), be a valuable component of the management team of your company and take advantage of all the resources, programs, and strategies available to you as a corporate executive. Doing so can also make you very attractive to the corporate recruiters out there with offers for more compensation and perks.

As a corporate executive, you should maximize your benefits and higher compensation … which means reading Chapter 2.

Main Takeaway Points

- Maximize your earnings … minimize your expenses … invest the difference.
- Set your target amount for financial independence.
- Focus your wealth-accumulation and growth approach to meet or exceed your target amount.

Resources

- Rescue Your Retirement with Paul Mladjenovic (the author's free retirement planning webinar for readers of this book) at … www.ravingcapitalist.com/rescue-your-retirement-webinar/
- The Retirement Café (www.theretirementcafe.com)
- Create a My Social Security account. www.ssa.gov/myaccount.
- Top 100 Retirement Blogs and Websites To Follow in 2021 (https://blog.feedspot.com/retirement_blogs/)
- American Association of Retired Persons (www.aarp.org)
- Association of Mature American Citizens (www.amac.us)
- 50 ideas for earning income in your spare time with Paul Mladjenovic—the author's free home business ideas for readers of this book at … www.ravingcapitalist.com/50-home-business-ideas-webinar/

CHAPTER 2

Executive Compensation

Your executive compensation and the financial resources available from your career choices form the foundation for your long-term investment success. This chapter and its resources will help you learn to develop build your wealth-building prowess to accelerate *your* financial independence.

Executive Wealth Building for Corporate Executives

Corporate executives have unique financial opportunities as well as some powerful tools for wealth building not available to most employees. Executive compensation packages, in addition to higher compensation, may include annual and long-term incentives (LTIs), stock options (restricted and unrestricted), deferred compensation, and bonuses based on company performance in addition to commission based on the performance of their individual business units.

In addition, executive perquisites (perks) can include special retirement plans, extra vacation, extra insurance plans, use of the company plane, company cars, club memberships, discounts, relocation services, closing costs, financial and legal counseling, and work/life coaching. There are powerful resources available that can help executives grow their money over the long term.

Often new executives are so focused on the success of their firm or enterprise that they neglect to maximize and leverage their executive benefits. It is often after several years that they will re-evaluate their approach, and some will seek out a qualified financial adviser for guidance.

Fast track your path to financial independence by maximizing corporate resources for *your* investment goals.

Executive compensation plans typically include access to personalized financial/estate/tax-optimization/insurance/personal liability planning— *use it!* This offering can boost your ability to grow wealth over time.

Programs that help executives grow their wealth are included here.

401k Plans

Maximizing the Company Match (It's More Complicated Than You Think)

Beware of the 401(a)(17) rule. There's a sneaky rule that trips up many corporate executives from maximizing their pre-tax 401k contributions. This rule stipulates that once an employee makes over $290k a year, the employer can no longer contribute a match to the 401k for them. Essentially the trick is to "frontload"—contribute more, earlier in the year, so that the full maximum pre-tax 401k contribution amount ($26,000 for age 50+ in 2021 tax year) is reached at the same time that the $290k earnings limit is reached, after which the company will be prevented from matching for the remainder of the year. If, like often happens, the executive tries to determine their contribution percentage by dividing $26k by the expected compensation, they will come up with a contribution rate that will cause much of his or her contributions to go unmatched, as they will have already hit the annual salary cutoff point by that time.

Of course, this also means that personal budgets must account for the fact that take-home pay will be less in the earlier part of each year and increase later in the year as the "frontloading" ends.

Choosing the Best 401k Asset Allocation

Busy executives often overlook how crucial asset allocation (choosing which funds to invest in within the 401k) can be to future wealth building. A performance advantage of even a few percentage points per year can literally add up to hundreds of thousands of dollars in retirement income over an investing lifetime. We have seen cases where executives sign up and began contributing to their 401k without even realizing that their contributions were "growing" in a default money-market fund, missing out on any market exposure or growth potential.

First, a traditional 40/60 mix of bond funds and stock/growth funds is often chosen by default as this "traditional" investment mix has embedded itself in financial culture. The reality, however, is that a young executive saving for a retirement perhaps 20, 30, or more years down the road should consider that, over longer timeframes, stocks have historically outperformed bonds by a wide margin. Remember also that bond prices benefit from lower interest rates and that, generally speaking, we are coming off a 30+ year decline in U.S. interest rates that began around 1980. (Your parents likely paid 16 to 18 percent if they took out a mortgage in the early 1980s, compared to as low as 2 percent in the late 2020.) The next few decades could have even more pronounced outperformance for stocks versus bonds if the tailwind that bonds have enjoyed turns into a headwind of slowly rising interest rates, as many financial experts expect.

So, what does this mean? We think executives with a 20+ year timeframe to retirement should consider placing 100 percent of their 401k contribution into "growth" or stock fund choices within their plan and minimizing or avoiding bond and "fixed" or money market choices entirely. This strategy can be particularly powerful as most 401k contributions are done on a regular basis which creates a built-in "dollar cost averaging" dynamic meaning that you will be buying more shares of each fund on periodic market dips as they inevitably occur. This is the smart persons' alternative to having a crystal ball and attempting to buy low and sell high, which research proves does not work for the vast majority of investors. This brings us to our third wealth-building strategy, which incidentally works for all investing accounts, but particularly for 401k:

Benign neglect: Take advantage of the market's upward bias. This may not seem like a powerful wealth builder, at first, but considering what we now know after analyzing decades of actual performance metrics in millions of real retirement accounts, it may well be the most important element discussed here.

The Dalbar organization has been publishing a survey of all reported 401k accounts since 1978 and the basic conclusion has been consistent for every 1-, 3-, 10-, or 20-year period analyzed: Americans are not good as market timers. They consistently buy high, and sell low, and this self-defeating behavior persists through all demographics, education backgrounds, and income levels. This is likened to planting a garden and then pulling up the plants every few weeks to see how the roots are growing. While markets have generally averaged around 10 percent per year over time, Dalbar indicates that there is a persistent "behavior gap" that costs most investors who attempt to change their fund mix due to economic or market expectations over 4 percent per year. That's a 40 percent reduction in performance due entirely to their own harmful behavior. Compounded over time, that "operator error" underperformance difference keeps growing to startling proportions. Sometimes boring is good. Once you've selected your asset allocation, hopefully focused on diversified stock growth funds (see Chapter 5 on mutual funds), benign neglect can potentially grow your nest egg 40 percent or more faster.

Deferred Compensation Programs/Long-Term Incentives

This plan withholds income until a specified time; in some cases the executive has an option of the length of time the compensation can be held. Examples of these plans include retirement plans, pensions, and employee stock options. In many cases, the company has a vesting period and if the executive leaves prior to that time, they forfeit the compensation.

The main advantage of deferred compensation plans is it reduces an individual's taxable income and can reduce exposure to the alternative minimum tax (AMT) while increasing the options of tax deductions.

Deferred compensation plans are one way to ensure an executive is retained, as leaving the firm may mean forfeiting the compensation.

Performance Bonus

These are bonuses paid based on the performance of given line of business or the profitability of the entire company (profit sharing). They can range from 2.5 to 7.5 percent but can be upward of 15 percent on top of base salary.

Sign-On Bonus

Once reserved for athletes and executives, these are more commonplace now when attracting top talent. It is a way to "buy out" compensation left on the table from a previous employer as well as establish goodwill with a new employee. These bonuses can have stipulations that protect the company's interest and large signing bonuses may be paid over a span of 12 to 18 months.

Retention Bonus/Change in Control Agreement

Especially during a merger and acquisition, or key projects, key executives are incented to provide continuity when there is uncertainty. This bonus encourages and motivates the executive/employee to stay and is usually between 10 and 15 percent of salary.

Stock Options

Stock options are an incentive to attract and retain valued employees and executives and are normally vested at 20 to 25 percent of the stock grant per year. From the taxman's point of view, options are not "property" before vesting, but exercising (the time when the holder purchases the stock) can create taxes for both incentive stock options and nonqualified stock options (NSO), the two classifications the vast majority fall under.

Executives granted NSOs (unless granted or "free"). But you should not go into debt to purchase stock options. Before purchasing, you should weigh the risk and ask yourself if this is money you can afford to lose. You should also only purchase stock options if you are confident that the company is going to continue to grow and profit.

You can exercise them before or after leaving your employer in most cases. You just have to follow the rules of your plan. If you decide to exercise the stock options, make sure you understand how they work. If you do this before you turn in your notice to leave the company, you keep your potential choices open. You need to be tax-smart to get the most out of your stock options. Stock options have been making a comeback after almost two decades out of favor. The dot-com (during 2000–2002) bust hurt executives who forgot that the market can go down as well as up. For more on stock options, refer to the sites listed in the resources at the end of this chapter.

Restricted stock. Restricted stock is another form of executive compensation offered by public companies. This is also presented as restricted stock units (RSUs). Restricted stock refers to corporate stock that is issued to personnel such as executives and directors but come with conditions. This stock is nontransferable and can only be traded in compliance with SEC rules covering this type of security. One of the major restrictions is that it may have a vesting period that will last a year or longer and it may stipulate that the stock's restrictions may be removed (giving the executive the opportunity to sell at market prices) after the executive has worked a specific length of time or until a specific date has been reached. Restricted stock is considered more valuable than stock options because it represents real wealth while stock options are only potential claims on wealth. Restricted stocks typically have a longer vesting period than corporate stock options. For more details, check out the resources at the end of this chapter.

Health Savings Accounts Paired With High Deductible Health Plan

As most know, the health savings account (HSA) can be used to pay for qualified medical expenses created in conjunction with high deductible health plans (HDHP). Contributions are made into the HSA by the employee and/or the employer up to the legal annual limit. The contributions can also be invested besides being able to pay for expenses such as medical, dental, optical, and prescription expenses.

Besides the fact that HSA has tax advantages (contributions are pre-tax), it also has a great retirement benefit that some do not realize since any unspent money is totally owned by the employee and this investable sum can be carried forward long term.

Additionally, the HSA is portable and the employee can continue to contribute to it (until you enroll in Medicare later on) even after leaving their employer.

Other Benefits and Programs to Consider

Lastly, discuss with your financial adviser and/or your human resource department the following items:

- Supplemental life insurance
- Split-dollar life insurance
- Supplemental disability insurance
- Long-term care insurance
- Job-related liability insurance

Main Takeaway Points

- Every corporate executive position offers programs and benefits that you can maximize to greatly enhance your wealth-building program.
- Before you accept a job offer, be aware of the programs, benefits, and typical compensation perks available to negotiate a stronger offer.
- Go to the resources below to learn more about gaining the greatest value from your position.

Note: Special thanks go to James Maendel of Maendel Wealth (www.maendelwealth.com/) and Frances M. Correa, corporate sales executive, for helping with the content of this chapter.

Resources

- Compensation Café (compforce.typepad.com/compensation_cafe/)
- The HR Capitalist (www.hrcapitalist.com/)
- HR Daily Advisor (hrdailyadvisor.blr.com/)
- CEO & Senior Executive Compensation Report for Private Companies (compreport.chiefexecutive.net/blog/)
- Employee Benefits Blog (www.employeebenefitsblog.com/)
- Compensation Resources (www.compensationresources.com/)

CHAPTER 3

Growth Stocks

For executives, it's hard to see a long-term path to future financial independence without stocks being an important part of the mix in the early going. Whether you are investing in stocks directly (such as in your stock brokerage account) or indirectly (such as through an exchange-traded fund or mutual fund), you will need to understand what they really are (vs. what you may read in popular financial sites), what their purpose is, and how to use them to achieve your financial objectives. Keep in mind that there are different types of stocks that can be applicable for different types of situations.

For the purpose of this book, I will keep the focus on stocks to grow your wealth (during your corporate executive career) and then switch to dividend-paying stocks for your later years when passive income is more suitable (retirement). Secondly, the focus is on long-term investing and not short-term speculating or trading.

The Plan

In a nutshell, here is "the plan" or blueprint I suggest for the stock portion of your portfolio going forward:

- In your early working years, have a mix of aggressive and conservative growth stocks.
- In your middle working years, move that mix to all conservative growth stocks.
- In your later working years (as you near retirement), start changing the mix to 50 percent dividend stocks and 50 percent conservative growth stocks.
- Whatever stocks you may have during your working years that do pay dividends, enroll in dividend reinvestment plans

(DRPs) offered by those dividend-paying companies. More on DRPs later in this chapter.

- Once the retirement years come, make sure the stock portion of your portfolio is fully dividend stocks. I will cover dividend stocks in the retirement income in Chapter 9.

"Stocks" Versus "Companies"

When you buy a stock, you are really buying partial ownership in a publicly traded company. It may sound somewhat obvious but it's not. Stocks (shares of stock) are bought and sold endlessly every day that the stock market is open and it is astonishing how many people buy stocks and don't realize that you are buying companies—the stock shares are merely a convenient way to participate. The point is that when you make the purchase your focus should be on the underlying company and the financial and market data (the "fundamentals") to help you analyze the company and make a rational decision about making it part of your investment portfolio.

Long Term Versus Short Term

The world of investing is really a long-term pursuit. When I say "long term" I do mean (ideally) five years or longer. If your timeframe is less than that, then stocks (especially those chosen for growth or "capital appreciation") may not have adequate time to bear profitable fruit. If your timeframe is one year or less, then avoid stocks. If your timeframe is two to five years, then you are better off with stocks that are more stable and also offer dividend income such as in public companies in industries such as utilities or consumer staples (also referred to as "defensive stocks").

Why five years? There is no magic in the timeframe beyond giving the marketplace adequate time to discover the gem you invested in so that market-buying interest propels the stock price to higher levels. One of my clients chose a "boring" water stock. Yet 10 years later, that stock was up 450 percent. That doesn't include the dividends that reliably came in quarter after quarter. The point is that quality stocks that grab the interest of the stock-buying public don't typically happen in a day or a week or a month. Reliable, quality companies ultimately attract greater interest over time, and your patience and diligence gets rewarded with huge percentage gains eventually. I recall one student from my class that bought a stock looking for a "quick killing" and then getting annoyed with a meager gain. Some years later he attended another class of mine and regretted not holding on to the stock as it grew by over 900 percent a few years later!

Just keep in mind that the time factor is more about giving your stock enough time to reach new heights as the market discovers it and not necessarily a strict condition of "calendar time."

Additionally, you need time since market and economic conditions change constantly. The folks that bought stocks right before the 2008 market crash saw their stocks plummet in the short term but with patience and discipline saw those same stocks hit all-time highs only a few short years later. Lastly, long-term investing is a much more assured way of achieving gains than trying to outmaneuver the market in the short term. Short-term trading and speculating is fraught with land mines as markets can "zig" as you "zag" and vice versa. I have seen all types of insanity in the short-term gyrations of the market. But in long-term investing, rational decisions do ultimately result in rational outcomes. Long term, the price of stocks of quality companies will zig-zag upward while the price of stocks of failing companies will zig-zag downward.

Given that, let's look at the "fundamentals," which tell you how strong the underlying company is and the prospects for a bright future for its stock.

Fundamental Analysis Versus Technical Analysis

When it comes to long-term investing, fundamental analysis or "looking at the fundamentals" is the name of the game. Yes, there is also "technical analysis" but that is more relevant for shorter term trading and/or speculating. Before we go further, let's define these terms.

Fundamental analysis looks at the company's financial strength and their standing in the industry/sector. Fundamental analysis looks at the company's profitability and sales data (such as their income statement) and the company's assets, liabilities, and net equity (such as on their balance sheet). Market data also comes into play as we look at the company's prospects in the industry and their market share. We also look at the company's numbers and analyze them to learn about the company's profitability, solvency, efficiency, and so on using ratios and other analytical tools.

Technical analysis looks more at the relatively short-term gyrations of the stock's price through the prism of price movements, charts, moving averages, trading volume data, and so on. While fundamental analysis focuses on the company, technical analysis focuses more on the stock's price and its movement especially over the short term (typically measured in days and weeks). It is beyond the scope of this book to get into greater details about these topics but there will be resources at the end of the chapter if you want to drill down on them. I will only focus on some key points in this chapter.

Because we are looking at long-term investing, I will only cover the most important fundamentals that are critical for success.

In a nutshell, fundamental analysis is about the "what," while technical analysis is about the "when." Fundamentals help determine what you will invest in for the long term while technical analysis helps you figure out when to buy or sell in the short term.

Key Fundamentals

Here are the main things I look at when I am deciding on the stock of a particular company:

1. Net profit. The net profit (total sales less total expenses as found in the company's income statement) is the single most important detail in the company's financial data. Don't just judge if the company had a profit in the most recent quarter or year ... make sure the company has consistent profitability over multiple years (three years or longer is preferable).

2. Positive net equity. The company's total assets are greater than the company's total liabilities. The greater the assets are versus the liabilities, the better. Seeing that the Net equity is positive over multiple periods (and hopefully growing) is a big plus.

3. Industry outlook. Is the company's industry strong and growing? A strong company in a strong industry with expected growth is ideal.

There ... kept it simple. Yes. There is more but these are the most important things I look at before I even consider a single share of their stock. Now let's look at some key ratios.

Key Fundamental Ratios

Ratios are simply numbers that have an important relationship to help you understand the strengths (or weaknesses) of the company's financial standing. Here are some I usually look at.

Price/Earnings Ratio

When I'm looking at a particular company, one of the most important ratios that I will look at is the price/earnings ratio. And it is something that I think everyone should be reviewing, especially if you're considering purchasing the stock of a company that is going to be in your portfolio for the long term, not only for the point of view of being a value-oriented approach, but also because it has a measure of safety; otherwise you might not realize that the price/earnings ratio is one of the few ratios that try to bridge those two worlds of the stock. As I mentioned earlier in this chapter, you have the stock and you have the underlying company.

Sometimes the stock will act without logic or reason in the marketplace in a given trading day or week. And what seems like erratic and uncoupled ways from the stock from the company itself. The Company is what we all know: it's a physical entity, by and large; even if it's an online company, you have people, you have products, you have services, you have financial statements, you have an enterprise, a physical enterprise, and the company is what you're actually looking at when you are thinking about investing.

Don't confuse investing and investors with the people out there who do things such as day trading, or swing trading, or speculating and using technical analysis and jumping in and jumping out. That's a different animal altogether. And I don't think that's really an appropriate pursuit, certainly not in this book. And if the corporate executives want to do the trading and jumping in and jumping out, you know that's a form of speculation, really, and there's nothing wrong with that. But again, it's outside the scope and purpose and goals of this particular book. I believe that long-term investing is a more assuring way of going forward. I've seen too often that people, whether they are corporate executives or common investors, or hedge funds have just gone into the excess and traded with companies and ended up losing thousands or millions or even billions. And if all they did was to view the stock through the prism, what about what investors should be viewing, which is the company itself, its sales, its profits, its prospects in the marketplace; we want to look at the company. But of course, to participate with the company, you ultimately have to buy the stock. And sometimes you have situations where the company is solid and good, but the stock price goes down (temporarily).

Or you'll see situations where the company is not that short of a footing, maybe it is even in financial difficulty, yet its stock price goes up. So the short term tends to be very irrational. But what you end up finding out is that a solid company ultimately will see value in its stock over the long term. In other words, the value of the company and the value of the stock, ultimately, in the long term, come to a mutual point. Bad companies ultimately will see their stocks go down in the long term; good companies will ultimately see their stocks zig-zagging upward in the long term. So finding tangible solid relationships between the stock and the company is very important. For me as a speculator sometimes, I'll see companies where, you know, they're in dreadful financial shape losing money, yet I see their stock price go up in the short term. So as far as I'm concerned, I consider it in an exit situation, a selling opportunity to get out, because ultimately long term the stock and the company value will be at parity to some extent. So, why is the price/earnings ratio an important feature?

Because here we look at the relationship between the price of the stock and the earnings or net earnings of the company, and we do so on a per share basis. In other words, if you see a company, for example, as a million shares of stock and, and the stock price is, let's say, $10 a share just to keep it simple. We know that the market value of the company is

$10 million. But the price per share is $10. Now, let's say this company makes a million dollars in net earnings. In other words, maybe it had $8 million in total sales and got $7 million in total expenses. So therefore, its net income is one million dollars. So here comes an easy example. If you're talking about a million shares, at $10 a share, and you're talking about a million dollars net profit for the company. Now you know that on a per share basis, the stock is $10 per share. And on a per share basis, the earning of the company is $1 earnings per share. So now you have a *P/E* ratio of 10. And that is, of course, a very low *P/E* ratio, but a very desirable ratio. And it's not typical of companies that were in a bear market where the stock market has fallen tremendously, but the company still has tangible value in earnings. So the price has come down.

Now, here's what you start to think about. Let's give you some parameters. What is generally a good price/earnings ratio? Well, by and large, a price/earnings ratio of less than 25 is desirable, because of how much you are willing to pay for the company; sometimes you'll see companies out there with a price/earnings ratio of, you know, 50, 75, or 100; these are much higher; this means that you're paying more and more for the company for its net earnings. So now you start seeing the risks involved, the higher the *P/E* ratio, the greater the risk; there's a greater chance that this might pull back, or the stock price may decline, in event of economic conditions changing and so forth. So for the sake of safety, and from a value-oriented approach, you want to be able to buy the stock of a company where the company has growing sales and earnings year in year out. But it has a fair valuation. Now I give you a minimum of 25. But again, you might talk to 10 different analysts; someone will tell you that under 50 is good. Still others might have a more stringent idea and say no, which should be 15 or less. But I think you get the point: if you had to choose between two companies, and these two companies were in the same industry, both profitable. And all things considered, they were generally equal as companies, but one had a very high stock price and the other one had a low stock price. And I mean, from a point of view of a price/earnings ratio, you'll find out that a price/earnings ratio, say, 25 is a much more fair valuation; you know what you're paying for those earnings of the company. Basically, if the *P/E* ratio was, say, 200, there would be an issue. And typically, when you want to find out when stock market bubbles occur, P/E ratios go through the roof, where the price of the stock is in nosebleed territory much higher, where the earnings haven't changed that much, or they certainly haven't moved in conjunction with the stock price involved. So P/E ratios are very important. Now, take a look at the P/E ratio of a company that's losing money: let's say, for example, that the stock price of that company is $50 a share, but the company is losing money. Well, now you'll tend to see that it has no P/E ratio or those financial websites who might calculate it will show a negative P/E ratio. Well, here's the thing: if you are looking to invest in a company, and the stock of the company either doesn't have a P/E ratio or it has a negative P/E ratio—in other words, it's running the losses—well now you're not investing. This should be a red flag, maybe one of the biggest red flags out there, that you should be aware of. And so the P/E ratio is something I will be very aware of, because as a value investor, you want to be able to pay in accordingly. And make sure you're not bargaining, but certainly you're not getting so overpriced; overpriced stock, compared to a company, runs the greater risk in the event of a correction or a downturn or other shock to the financial system. These companies stand to lose a lot in their share value, and you want to be able to avoid that. So you should definitely be looking at the P/E ratio, and make sure that you know, especially if these are bad economic times, the P/E ratio should be low … preferably at or below 25. You can find low P/E ratios typically among more stable, reliable companies out there, like food and water than utilities as examples. There's nothing wrong with higher P/E ratios. Generally speaking, growth stocks tend to have a higher P/E ratio. And the reason is that many people will be buying the stock with the full expectations (or hope?) that the earnings will come; maybe they're investing in a company. They feel like this is a hot new technology or hot new service, or the product or service is in vogue right now. And everybody loves it, as there is opportunity for expanding sales and profits, in the near future, and hopefully for the extended future. So, there's nothing wrong with that. But my feeling is that if you're paying excessive amounts like say north of a P/E ratio of 100 now, you have to worry; there is a chance that when the reality does hit, the stock price has an even shot of coming down very much so. This is why whenever I look at someone's portfolio with them, and I see some very high *P/E* ratio stock or stocks that want to get away with losses, one of the first things I tell them to do is: do you really need that stock? Maybe you should consider selling some or most of it; at the very least, why not consider putting in stop loss orders or trailing stops and make them good till cancelled (GTC). That way, you can be able to go into this particular stock with your eyes wide open and discipline things such as stop loss orders or, my favorite type of order, trailing stops.

These are the types of things that will limit the downside without limiting the upside. So the bottom line is look at the *P/E* ratios and if you are in very high *P/E* ratio stock, which again is fine, be more cautious about it and put in place disciplined approaches such as trailing stops to continue to maximize the gains, hopefully watching zig-zag upward. But in the meanwhile, make sure you're protecting against the downside risk and approaching things in a very disciplined way, with your long-term wealth-building plan remaining intact.

Debt-to-Asset Ratio

This solvency ratio is simple but I check all the time. You obviously want a company with a strong balance sheet where total assets are significantly greater than total liabilities. If a company's total assets are $2 billion and their total liabilities are $1 billion, then the ratio of debt to assets is 50 percent. If you invest in a company where total liabilities exceed total assets, then you are not investing ... you are speculating. Solvency is critical, especially during recessions or bad economic times.

Comparative Year Ratios

This type of ratio is about consistency regarding the company's primary financial over multiple years. You want a company that shows, for example, growth in net income from year 1 to year 2 and on to year 3. The same should be with total sales and with the company's net shareholder equity (meaning total assets less total liabilities to derive the company's net worth or net equity). Successful companies are not about success in a single year: they are about consistently doing well in their key fundamentals year after year.

Growth Versus Income Stocks

When we talk about the classes of stocks that you're going to invest in, there are many to consider but the main ones that fit your goals, both the short term and the long term, are growth stocks and income stock. Growth stocks are about stocks that are well positioned for steady growth in the coming months and years; in other words you're looking at capital appreciation or capital gain potential. Income stocks are referred to as stocks that have the potential to give you steady dividend income that can happen now and in the foreseeable future. In this chapter, I cover growth stocks. I will cover dividend stocks (also called "income stocks") in Chapter 9.

Both of these have a strong purpose in your portfolio and you should be spending a lot of time analyzing these or choosing the advice of financial experts that specialize in these types of securities. In your working years, the focus of your portfolio should be on growth: you want your money growing so that it reaches the point that the total asset value of your portfolio has the ability to be converted to the point that it can give you dividend growth so that you can benefit from dividend income that will rise especially in times of inflation which can be a significant risk for retirees.

How to Choose a Growth Stock

If you see the views of 100 stock-picking geniuses, you could easily get 10 different ideas about how to choose that "hot stock" with blistering growth potential. Just keep in mind that a huge part of the picture is outside your view: there is no crystal ball or sure-fire way to choose a "hot stock" since we must understand the fundamental reason why a stock rises or falls.

When there are more buyers (or buying transactions) for a given stock, supply and demand will push the stock price upward. The reverse is also true … when there are more sellers than buyers, the stock price will fall. This market dynamic is in play every day that the stock market is open for trading.

You can choose the stock of a great company and its price could go nowhere in the near term or even decline. You could choose the stock of a poorly run company and see the stock price irrationally shoot upward. You can't avoid the fact that the stock's rise or fall is based on factors that may seem uncontrollable or unforeseeable which is the machination of the marketplace. Given that reality, how do you actually choose a stock with winning potential?

The most important consideration when choosing a growth stock is that the underlying company has strong fundamentals and is a recognized leader in a growing industry or sector.

The best way to proceed with choosing that potential growth stock is to view the knowable factors tied to that stock (analyzing the company itself) and how well positioned it is in a sector or industry that is in demand now and logically in the foreseeable future.

Growth Strategies With Dividend Stocks

One of my favorite strategies for long-term growth is to take advantage of those public companies that have the above features I just covered and also a DRP which many dividend stocks have. To qualify for that company's DRP it is a simple criteria: you have to be a stockholder of record, meaning that you own one or more shares of the company's stock. Whether you have one share or 1,000, I think that enrolling in that public company's DRP should be a strong consideration. The main reason is that you can more quickly compound and grow your stock holdings which will grow your share total to the point that you will have a great potential dividend income in your later years when you cease reinvesting the dividends and change to receiving your income to cover the costs of being retired.

Most DRPs have two valuable features:

1. As the name states, these types of stocks give you the ability to reinvest your dividends into the common stock of the public company instead of receiving the dividend as a cash payout. This is where the "reinvestment" feature comes in. If you don't need the money (and

you plan on owning the stock for the foreseeable future), reinvesting the dividends will make a lot of sense.

2. The second common feature is "optional cash payments." This means that you have the option of sending money into the DRP to purchase more shares without paying commissions or other fees.

I think that DRPs are an excellent (and relatively conservative) way to grow your stock holdings in a given public company. Imagine starting at, say, 100 shares and over time through reinvestment and small periodic cash contributions it will result in having 500 shares giving you a fatter dividend (most dividend-paying companies tend to regularly increase their dividend pay-outs over time).

Insider Stock Strategies

As a corporate executive you can buy the stock of your own company (if it's a public company) and for most executives this is the best place to start in the world of stock investing. When you are an insider, you have a bird's eye view into the operations of the company and its prospects. If the company is doing well, then it makes sense to consider buying some of it, given your ability to understand it more intimately than the general public. Just make sure you discuss with the company's legal department regarding any responsibilities you have about insider reporting. Secondly, remember to diversify. I knew one executive that had over $1 million worth of his company's stock and little else at the time of his retirement. That is too concentrated and can become a financial hazard if anything goes wrong with the company. Discuss this with your financial adviser regarding appropriate diversification.

Tactics for Safety

Successful stock investing is not just what you buy and when you buy the stock; it is also about how you do it. Check out with your broker's customer service department or their website about getting proficient about brokerage orders that add safety and discipline to your investing approach such as:

- *Stop loss order.* If you have a stock at $50 per share and you are concerned about it declining in the near term, you can, for example, put on a stop loss order at $45 and make it Good 'til Cancelled (GTC). This means that if the stock falls and hits $45, it will automatically be sold so you can prevent further losses. This order doesn't limit the upside, but it does limit the downside. GTC means that the order will stay on indefinitely until either you cancel it or it hits the brokerage firm's maximum time limit (typically 60, 90, or 120 days).

- *Trailing stop order.* I like this even more. Here you designate a dollar amount or a percentage amount similar to a stop loss order but this order will ride upward with the stock price but stay frozen in the event the stock price reverses and heads down. In other words, when the stock price rises, so does the price level of the trailing stop by your designated amount such as $5 below the stock price or 10 percent. At a stock price of $30, the trailing stop could be at $27 (10 percent in this example). If the stock rises to $40, then the trailing stop rises to $36 (the same 10 percent). If the stock declines at this point, the trailing stop stays at $36. If it is triggered then you will get out at the sale price of $36. The trailing stop order is great for letting the stock price rise with no limits, but it raises the lower limit to protect more and more of your gain.

- *Other tactics.* Discuss with your financial adviser other techniques and strategies for maximizing gains and minimizing losses. Many experienced investors use call and put options to add more control and safety to their growth stock strategies.

Main Takeaway Points

- Consider picking stocks of companies that have strong fundamentals (growing sales and profits, low debt, etc.) that are considered leaders in a growing sector or industry.
- Focus on growth stocks during your working years and switch to dividend stocks during your later years when you are focused on retirement.

Stock Investing Resources

- *Stock Investing for Dummies* (6th edition) by Paul Mladjenovic, published by Wiley
- Investopedia (www.investopedia.com)
- Market Watch (www.marketwarch.com)
- Nasdaq (www.nasdaq.com)
- Investing.com (www.investing.com)

CHAPTER 4

Exchange-Traded Funds (ETFs)

Exchange-traded funds (ETFs) are mutual funds that you can buy (or sell) as easily as you can a stock, hence the "exchange traded" part of their names. I like the ease to buy an entire portfolio of, say, food and beverage stocks in my stock brokerage account with a few mouse clicks which is just as easy as buying shares in a single food and beverage company. ETFs do compare favorably with mutual funds but there are some key distinctions. I think that ETFs can play a major role in the corporate executive's long-term wealth-building program.

ETFs Versus Mutual Funds

There are two primary differences between ETFs and regular conventional mutual funds. The first difference is that although both of them manage portfolios, the mutual fund portfolio is actively managed, while the ETF portfolio is typically a static portfolio. In other words, if I was going to get an energy mutual fund and an energy ETF, for example, whereas both of them would invest in the energy sector, the energy mutual fund portfolio would regularly be rotated; they would be buying, selling, and holding, and it would want to keep on moving forward in that regard. So it might have the top, say, 50 energy securities, but the investment management team for this mutual fund may say, "A company in our portfolio is no longer meeting our criteria for staying in the portfolio." Given that, they may reduce the position or they may sell the entire position outright.

The ETF, meanwhile, typically tends to have a static portfolio. An energy ETF, for example, might have the top 50 or 60 energy companies in that sector. It gets predicated and structured at the inception of the ETF. Beyond that, the only time that a transaction would occur is if there is a material change in a particular company such as if there is a merger, a takeover, or the stock is no longer trading (such as being delisted as a publicly trading security). One advantage of the static portfolio in the ETF is that it tends to keep fees relatively low, certainly lower than the ongoing transaction and management fees and costs that are typical in an actively traded mutual fund.

So that's the first major difference between ETFs and mutual funds. The second major difference is the method of transacting it. When you're investing in mutual fund, you're typically purchasing in dollar amounts such as $1,000 or $5,000 or whatever amounts are stipulated by that specific mutual fund. Usually mutual funds are purchased directly from the mutual fund company but in recent years more mutual funds have also opted to have their shares have the ability to be transacted inside regular brokerage or individual retirement accounts. There may or may not be transaction fees associated with the purchase (or sale) so consult with your broker for details.

Meanwhile, purchasing ETFs is similar to purchasing stock. You can buy a few shares—or 50 or 100—but it is still easily done through your broker's website inside your regular brokerage or individual retirement account. Beyond those two major differences, the only remaining essential difference is transaction costs. With ETFs, the transaction can be simple. With mutual funds the transaction fees can be a little more complicated and there are more details in the chapter on mutual funds (Chapter 5).

A Simple Approach With ETFs

In your working years, choose ETFs that focus on growth, both general growth and specific sector growth. A simple example of doing this is to choose an ETF that mirrors the Nasdaq (for aggressive growth) and another choice could be an ETF that mirrors the S&P 500 stock index (for conservative growth). Additionally, a good consideration would be some ETFs that focus on a particular sector such as tech stocks, energy, or health care. Start as early in your career as possible to get into and continue to add to those ETFs that offer long-term growth prospects. The bulk of your growth-oriented portfolio should be conservative growth (especially in your later working years). The sooner you start, the less you will need to be doing speculative or aggressive securities and strategies "trying to catch up."

In your retirement years or in the timeframe just prior to your retirement years, you should be focused on ETFs (and/or large-cap stocks) that have income through dividends along with the potential for dividend growth. As you near retirement, you're best off focusing or reshuffling your portfolio so that you're doing less growth and more into sectors that have stability and income potential. Some examples of this are consumer staples, food and beverage, and utilities. More about dividend-oriented ETFs in the chapter on retirement income (Chapter 9).

S&P 500

The two aspects of your investing career, which is again growth in the first part, then later on, presumably during your retirement years, you're looking for income, can be easily fashioned with popular ETFs. In separate sections, we spoke about ETFs that are in individual sectors: you can get an ETF for consumer staples or ones that cover utilities or commodities. These ETFs cover specific sectors or subsectors (industries). Health care, for example, is a broad and diversified sector from an investment point of view. But within this broad sector are segments that have different characteristics and can perform differently in the same given economic conditions. The health care sector has segments that are cyclical (moving up and down with the primary economic "up and down" cycles) such as medical technology. But it also has defensive segments such as pharmaceuticals and drug retailers which don't necessarily do well as the economy grows but they are more resilient during recessions and downturns. An ETF that mirrors the S&P 500 index does not reflect a particular sector or subset of industries; rather it will invest in those companies that have met the specific criteria of being in one of the most widely watched stock market index created and overseen by Standard and Poor's (www.spglobal.com/ratings/en/).

For a list of all the companies in the S&P 500 index, go to https://markets.businessinsider.com/index/components/s&p_500?op=1.

Having an ETF that mirrors the S&P 500 index of companies can be an anchor or long-term cornerstone of your growth since there are few better ways of getting broad, conservative market exposure than the S&P 500. The Dow Jones industrial average (DJIA) is more widely watched and reported but it only tracks 30 of the largest and representative companies and there are certainly ETFs that mirror this indicator (such as the ETF with the symbol "DIA") but they may not be the optimal choice for conservative growth. To choose the S&P 500, here are three ETFs that track it:

- SPDR S&P 500 ETF (SPY)
- iShares Core S&P 500 ETF (IVV)
- Vanguard S&P 500 ETF (VOO)

The strength and diversification of the S&P 500 makes it a no-brainer as a long-term component of your conservative growth portfolio. The diversification isn't just among 500 strong, well-capitalized companies; it has diversification among a strong cross section of sectors and industries.

When the moment comes to switch gears from growth to a focus on income, you can sell all or a portion of these ETFs with a few mouse clicks and easily move into income-oriented ETFs. If you have SPY, for example, then why not switch to SPDR S&P Dividend ETF (SDY)? You would still have the power of the S&P 500 but you would go from SPY's 1.33 percent dividend yield (as of June 2021) to SDY's heftier 2.51 percent dividend yield to nearly double your dividend income. Of course, I think you can do even better with other dividend income ETFs but if you want to stick to the relatively greater safety of the S&P 500 and still improve the income, you have options such as this.

Sector Rotation With ETFs

Using ETFs for sector rotation is actually a great way over the long term to keep your account growing based on the economy's business cycles. And let me just use a very modest example. There are ETFs that are in consumer discretion, which is a sector and there are ETFs in consumer staples, which is also a sector. Consumer discretion is based on people's wants and generally speaking consumer staples are based on people's needs, I personally have a bias on consumer staples. People will always be buying things that they need. But of course, when the economy is doing well, consumer discretion tends to do better. So what corporate executives could do is generally see if the outlook for the economy looks good, based on their own observations, plus their research on the main financial websites and the headlines from financial publications. If the feeling is that the economy is doing well and moving into a period of optimism and growth, then it pays to have more of your money in as a percentage of your portfolio in consumer discretion. Because as the economy does well, as the job picture brightens, as the GDP grows, that means more and more people are doing well, more and more people are able to take their disposable income and invest in things that they want to invest in. So good examples of this would be, restaurants or vacation and entertainment; more people will be doing these things. Whereas think of the reverse: if the economic clouds tend to darken, and you start seeing this contraction, you can even see within the scope of your own business, if things are getting tighter, total sales are slowing. And the corporate executive can take a look at the microcosm of their corporation, and then juxtapose it against the research and the headlines and the financial publications covering the general economy. If the economy looks like it's shrinking, contracting, you know the company's sales are also slowing down. The GDP is not growing as normally as it would be, and people are starting to worry about pullbacks, more businesses closing, and so forth. So when the economy looks negative, then what happens at that point? Then people react accordingly in the economy. They are much less apt to be putting their money into luxuries and "wants." They will be saving their money, and the greater percentage of their spending will be going into things they need. Necessities … and the company that produce them … become paramount. Given that, the consumer staples sector tend to do well. So as a recap, the bottom line is when the economy is growing and doing well—consumer discretion— the consumer discretionary sector tends to do well. And when economy is contracting, or looking negative, then consumer staples tend to do well. So for corporate executives, it's not that difficult a task in terms of allocating investment capital. And it's not short term, jumping in and jumping out and speculating. A sector rotation is by and large a very reliable way of investing over the macro picture going forward months and possibly years. So, in this very simple example, you can be able to then invest accordingly; you can be able to invest in ETFs or mutual funds that are into consumer discretionary, in the event of a growing or optimistic economy. Or if the economy tends to look negative and pessimistic by and large, then there would be a shift away from consumer discretionary ETFs and mutual funds and into consumer staples ETFs and mutual funds. So this is a very valid and acceptable example. And it's a way, for the corporate executive, to keep on building wealth without worrying about choosing individual stocks. You can have an easier time seeing the outcome or seeing the expectations for a given sector and then shifting their money accordingly to keep their portfolio growing in both good times and bad.

Sectors and ETF Choices

Choosing a winning sector is much easier (and safer) than trying to choose a winning stock so this section will be important to your overarching wealth-building plan. I have listed below the primary sectors along with a description regarding their main investment purposes (for your goals) along with a representative ETF (and their symbols in parenthesis). Don't take this as advice, of course, but please do your due diligence before you make any investment choices, and consulting a trusted financial adviser is highly recommended.

Agriculture. This sector encompasses the world of commodities such as grains and cotton. This is not typically treated as a sector among the major financial sites, but in the world of ETFs, it is a vital area. Agricultural ETFs tend to perform well during inflationary times especially when demand is strong and the economic outlook is bullish. Examples of agricultural ETFs are:

- DBC
- DBA
- MOO

Communication services. This sector has companies involved in telecommunications, entertainment, and broadband and Internet services.

It tends to be cyclical and is a good consideration when the economy is on a growth path or expanding. Examples of Communication ETFs are:

- Vanguard Telecom ETF (VOX)
- iShares US Telecommunications ETF (IYZ)
- iShares Global Telecom ETF (IXP)

Consumer discretionary. This ETF is about "consumer wants" and is very sensitive to the economy's ebbs and flows. The companies here offer goods and services tied to consumer technology, restaurants, travel, and vacation. The best time to invest here is when the economy is rebounding and growing and consumer confidence is generally positive. Examples of ETFs are:

- Consumer Discretionary Select Sector SPDR (XLY)
- Consumer Discretionary AlphaDEX Fund (FDX)
- Vanguard Consumer Discretion ETF (VCR)

Consumer staples. This sector is tied to "consumer needs" and it is a sector I personally favor as a core portfolio presence. Think of what people need, no matter how good or bad the economy is. Companies here offer food, beverage, clothing, and other personal need-related products and services. When the economy is contracting, uncertain, or in a recession, this sector shines and the stocks in this sector tend to be of low volatility. Examples of ETFs include:

- Consumer Staples Select Sector SPDR (XLP A)
- Consumer Staples AlphaDEX Fund (FXG B+)
- Vanguard Consumer Staples ETF (VDC A+)

Energy. This sector has companies involved in the exploration, production, and management of oil, gas, and other energy-related commodities. When the economy is growing and doing well, demand for energy is strong and rises, so energy-related ETFs do well. Examples of energy ETFs are:

- Energy Select Sector SPDR (XLE)
- SPDR S&P Oil & Gas Exploration & Production ETF (XOP)
- Vanguard Energy ETF (VDE)

Financials. This sector includes banks, brokerage firms, and mortgage and insurance companies. Companies in the financial sector are engaged in businesses such as banking and brokerage, mortgage finance, and insurance. This sector is very sensitive to macro events such as economic cycles and changes to interest rates and federal regulatory and fiscal policies. This sector does well when the economy is growing and interest rates are stable. Diminish your presence here when economic and financial market difficulties are imminent. Examples of ETFs include:

- Financial Select Sector SPDR Fund (XLF)
- Vanguard Financials ETF (VFH)
- SPDR S&P Bank ETF (KBE)

Health care. This diversified sector can be a long-term holding during good and bad times since health care tends to be a constant necessity. This sector includes hospitals, pharmaceuticals, drug retailers, and medical device manufacturers. Examples of ETFs include:

- Health Care Select Sector SPDR (XLV)
- Nasdaq Biotechnology ETF (IBB)
- Vanguard Health Care ETF (VHT)

Industrials. The industrials sector includes companies that are manufacturers of capital goods and heavy machinery in areas such as construction and engineering, electrical equipment, and infrastructure. This sector performs well during times of economic growth and expansion but lags during recessions and slow growth. Examples of ETFs include:

- Industrial Select Sector SPDR (XLI)
- Vanguard Industrials ETF (VIS)
- iShares Transportation Average ETF (IYT)

Information technology. This sector includes companies that provide computer hardware, software, semiconductors, cloud computing, and technology consulting services. In terms of market value, this is a large and volatile sector since it includes big-name tech firms and performs well when the economy is expanding. Examples of ETFs include:

- Technology Select Sector SPDR (XLK)
- Vanguard Information Tech ETF (VGT)
- DJ Internet Index Fund (FDN)

Materials. This sector has companies involved in processing chemicals, plastics, and mining for precious and base metals and minerals. The materials sector is sensitive to the economic cycle and typically performs well during an economic expansion. Examples of ETFs include:

- Materials Select Sector SPDR Fund (XLB)
- Vanguard Materials ETF (VAW)
- iShares U.S. Basic Materials ETF (IYM)

Real estate. This sector is composed of companies that own and manage commercial and residential real estate properties. Many of the companies are real estate investment trusts ("REITs" and they are more fully covered in Chapter 6). Real estate investments can offer a diversified addition to your portfolio versus stocks and bonds. This area's potential is tied to the general real estate market and has benefits such as being an inflation hedge with the potential for relatively high income. Examples of ETFs include:

- Vanguard REIT ETF (VNQ)
- Vanguard Global ex-U.S. Real Estate Index Fund ETF (VNQI)
- Schwab U.S. REIT ETF (SCHH)

Utilities. The utilities sector includes companies that engage in the production and distribution of gas and electric power, water, and other utility services. Utilities sector is a stable sector and provides solid dividend income as well. This sector is considered a "go to" investment during periods of economic uncertainty or recessions. Some popular ETFs are:

- Utilities Select Sector SPDR (XLU)
- Vanguard Utilities ETF (VPU)
- First Trust Utilities AlphaDEX (FXU)

Sector ETFs are a solid way to position your portfolio during good times and bad, and rotating from one sector(s) to other sector(s) has proven to be a good way to be positioned during the broader up and down moves of the general economy.

Specialty ETFs

The previous section covers the primary sector ETF considerations but ETFs provide greater variety given your chosen approach to investment and speculative opportunities that you should consider discussing with your financial adviser. There are many opportunities with ETFs that offer a different slant or composition so that you can make more targeted choices in your investing or speculating approach. Here are some added potential choices:

Index ETFs. Earlier in this chapter we covered the S&P 500 index ETF (SPY) but there are also ETFs for the DJIA or the Nasdaq stock index (QQQ). These ETFs don't follow a sector but will structure the portfolio to mirror the stocks in a given index.

Leveraged bullish ETFs. Are you feeling really positive on a given sector, industry, or index? Then you can get ETFs that are "turbo-charged" with added securities (such as options) to be more aggressive. Of course, if the positions go against you (decline or worse) then the losses can also be magnified.

Bearish (or short) ETFs. Do you strongly believe that a given sector or index will be declining in the near future and you would like to profit from this decline? This is speculating, of course, but if you are game then look into ETFs that are structured to profit from those down moves in the underlying securities.

Dividend ETFs. These are ETFs with companies that offer high (or growing) dividends. These are covered more fully in Chapter 9.

Currency ETFs. Do you want to add currency opportunities to your portfolio? Are you feeling bullish on the U.S. dollar, the Euro, or the Yen? There are plenty of currency ETFs that you can choose from.

There are hundreds of ETFs to choose from, so head offer to the ETF sites listed below and start your research. I wish you success!

ETFs and Added Tactics and Benefits

As you can tell, I think that ETFs can be a powerful addition to your investing (or speculative) pursuits. Just to round out this chapter, here are some final points to keep in mind when you are considering ETFs:

- Many ETFs are optionable. This means that you can buy (or sell) call and/or put options on them. Selling (writing) call and put options on ETFs (or stocks) can be a great income strategy if done properly. More on this strategy in Chapter 9.
- You can do stop loss orders, limit orders, and/or trailing stop orders to enhance your transactions. Stop loss orders and trailing stop orders can add safety to your positions during volatile or declining markets.
- ETFs can be marginable. This means that you can have the ability to borrow against your ETFs and use those funds for another purpose. If, for example, you had $10,000 in marginable ETFs, you could borrow up to 50 percent and take the $5,000 and pay off some high-interest credit card debt. Just keep in mind that you should be very cautious and judicious when using borrowed funds so speak with your financial adviser about how suitable it is for you.

For the above tactics, speak to your stock brokerage's customer service department about the details for your individual account.

Main Takeaway Points

- ETFs are a convenient way to invest in sectors and industries in your portfolio.
- Learn which sectors rise and decline with the ebbs and flow of the economy and know which ETFs are appropriate.

Resources

- ETF DataBase (www.etfdb.com)
- ETF Guide (www.etfguide.com)
- ETF Channel (www.etfchannel.com)

All three resources provide searchable databases of ETF along with news, education, and ETF analysis. Additionally, many major financial websites have extensive coverage of ETFs such as MarketWatch (www.marketwatch.com), Investopedia (www.investopedia.com), and Bloomberg (www.bloomberg.com).

CHAPTER 5

Mutual Funds

When a corporate executive is busy running an enterprise or an important department or component of a larger enterprise (such as a publicly traded company), he or she shouldn't have to worry about every investment decision … a mutual fund is much like outsourcing a portion of your funds to an investment portfolio professional for them to perform the daily, ongoing task of overseeing and managing an investment portfolio and regularly making the decision to buy, sell, or hold a given security for that portfolio. There are thousands of funds to choose from, so your task is to choose the right fund (or set of funds) so that they can serve your long-term goals with their portfolio choices.

What Is a Mutual Fund?

A mutual fund is a pool of money that is managed by investment firm. This pool of money is invested in a portfolio of securities by the investment firm. This portfolio of securities is intended to reach a particular goal such as growth or income or preservation of capital.

A mutual fund's main benefits are that it offers professional investment management, diversification, and convenience. One of the main risks is that a mutual fund is only as good as the value of its portfolio's holdings (assets and securities). After all, a mutual fund is a conduit and it is the value and performance of its portfolio that will matter over the long term. This chapter is there to guide you to proper selections to serve your future needs.

In my experience, the primary mistake that investors make is choosing the wrong category in the first place. The second mistake is making a poor mutual fund choice once you are inside any given category. I will address both issues in this chapter … first the categories.

The Nine Basic Mutual Fund Investment Objectives

In the world of mutual funds, the corporate executive doesn't need to make the choice of an individual security or a group of securities in a portfolio; the choice boils down to making the right (or at the very least the most appropriate) mutual fund choice that fits your needs at that given time and for your given purposes.

Mutual funds by and large will be mostly in your retirement accounts such as in your 401k plan so they tend to be long-term commitments (unless you assert your choices and concerns with the administrator). Typically, if you're working for a corporation, they're going to be working with their chosen plan administrator, and they have a family of funds, or a universe of funds to select with. So in some cases, you might not be able to choose a mutual fund outside of this universe of selections, and the universe is going to depend on the administrators: some administrators may only have a dozen choices or so while others may provide you with a broader menu of options. The bottom line is that it's good to choose mutual funds, from a point of view of whether it fits in your current situation, given the economic conditions at the time and the prospects for upcoming economic conditions.

Let's go in depth and figure out about the nine basic categories of mutual funds. If you can at least get to the right category that's the bulk of your journey. By and large, during your working years, your funds should be generally growth oriented, whether it's conservatively or aggressively growth oriented. You may not need to be 100 percent in growth because of any other factors in your situation but at least 75 to 80 percent of your investable assets should be growth oriented. It stands to reason that if you don't need the cash, and hopefully, if you're managing your day-to-day inflow and outflow (income and expenses) well, then you won't need to touch these funds. And they should be left alone so that over the months and years during your tenure as in your corporate position, that money should grow as much as possible.

The three main categories of mutual funds are aggressive growth, conservative growth, and growth and income. Then there are three main income categories which are aggressive income, conservative income, and tax-free income (municipal bond). The final three categories are basically specialty categories which include sector funds, international funds, and money market funds.

All of these main categories will have subcategories. International mutual funds, for example, have subcategories such as "international growth funds," "international income funds," and (you guessed it) "international growth and income funds."

Any one of those can serve an optimal purpose, again, given your current situation and what the situation looks like in the general economy and the financial markets. Alright, so let's rattle them off one at a time.

Aggressive Growth Fund

Everybody loves the idea of finding that one great stock that soars from under $5 per share to triple digits in a short time. The problem is that for every new, hot small-cap company that soars, there may be 20 or 50 that go nowhere (or go out of business). It is a better bet to choose a well-managed aggressive growth mutual fund which will use their full-time expertise and research to pick a portfolio of 40–50–60 stocks with great potential. If only a fraction of them soar by triple or quadruple percentage gains, then the overall portfolio will do well. Aggressive growth mutual funds will tend to focus on small-cap and/or micro-cap stocks since they have the greatest potential for growth.

Phrases such as "small cap," "mid cap," and "large cap" are references to market capitalization which means that particular public company's market value. If a company's stock is $20 per share and it has 10 million shares outstanding, then its market cap is $200 million (10 million shares times $20 per share). Small-cap stocks tend to have a market capitalization of under $1 billion (give or take a few million).

When you look at any mutual fund, the main document is the fund prospectus and it will reveal the objective of the fund and what types of securities it invests in. It will also provide a recent snapshot of the portfolio so you can see what stocks (or other securities) are in the fund's portfolio. Reading the fund objective which is usually a brief paragraph often on the first page of the prospectus will tell you immediately whether you should consider investing in the fund. You can ask yourself "does this fund's objective match my own objective?"

In the case of an aggressive growth mutual fund, the fund's objective will communicate that it will basically be either speculation, aggressive growth, or maximize capital gains and appreciation which is a typical language for an aggressive growth mutual fund. Keep in mind that the prospectus will give you a succinct education on the fund including details such as fund's performance, management's brief resumes, fund fees, and other pertinent information. The fund's managers will seek and invest in companies that may be obscure today but may become tomorrow's Google or Microsoft. Remember that this is the kind of fund that you should have a minimum of 5 to 10 years to be in, so it has adequate time to grow. The problem with aggressive growth is that it tends to be very sensitive to economic cycles. When the economy is booming, this kind of fund has the potential to lead the pack among all the mutual fund categories upward. However, when the economy (or financial market) is crashing or recessionary, then this fund might be one of the worst ones to be in. This is one of the main reasons that you need a long time horizon so that the fund has time to grow and zig-zag upward.

I think that if a corporate executive has adequate funds and is 10 to 20 years away from retirement, having a portion of your portfolio in such a fund is not a bad idea. But it's not necessary to have a huge portion of your personal portfolio in aggressive choices (no more than 10 or 20 percent is more than adequate). And even that amount of exposure should be greatly reduced as you approach pre-retirement years.

If you are keeping your overall spending under control during your working years and maximizing both your retirement plan contributions and your after-tax investing in regular brokerage accounts, then wealth accumulation should not be difficult and you can focus more on conservative growth strategies ... starting with the next category.

Conservative Growth Mutual Fund

Conservative growth mutual funds (as well as conservative growth ETFs covered in Chapter 4) should be primary workhorses in your long-term wealth-building approach.

Conservative growth mutual funds tend to choose stocks of companies that have a proven track record of growth. If you checked their portfolio (either in their recent market snapshot or at their website), you will likely see companies you are familiar with and they are likely market leaders in their sectors industries. For this category, the fund objective might say something along the lines of "seeking long-term appreciation in established growth companies," with a primary emphasis on capital gain or appreciation, and a minimal objective when it comes to income. Some of these securities may have dividends, but whether they have them or not is not the primary concern. They're looking for companies that have the ability to outgrow their peers in that particular industry or sector. So conservative growth mutual funds should play a large and active role in your long-term picture. You know, it should be there right in the middle of your 401k plan or IRA portfolios ... hopefully among several conservative growth mutual funds that are at or near the top of their category. There is another category I like which is next.

Growth and Income Mutual Funds

The third category is growth and income. This means that the funds in this category have the dual objectives of both growth and income. This category can be broken down into several subcategories.

Equity income mutual fund. An equity income fund will have a portfolio that is 80 percent or in stocks. So you see where the growth comes from, because obviously, stocks are considered a primary generator of growth. But where is the income coming from? Well, in equity income, the stocks do double-duty by paying higher than average dividends (usually 3 percent yield or higher). These stocks are usually referred to as "income stocks" or "dividend stocks." Most stocks out in the general stock market may either have a low dividend (typically 2 percent or less) or no dividend at all. These dividend-paying stocks tend to be large, established companies with good cash flows and that usually do not need to finance major projects or finance or acquire other assets (such as taking over another company). The bottom line is that dividend stocks would be providing both the growth and the income. This subcategory is one of my personal favorites because if you choose the distribution option of "total reinvestment" for all distributions in the fund (meaning dividends, interest, and capital gains), the long-term compounding affect gives this category strong appeal and growth prospects.

Balanced mutual fund. The other major subcategory is the balanced mutual fund. It is called so because it manages to strike a balance of both stocks and bonds in the portfolio. At any given time, it will be 40 to 60 percent in one and the remainder in the other. It will seek growth from the stocks and income from the bonds. If the managers believe that the unfolding environment will be good for stocks, then the portfolio could be 60 percent stocks and 40 percent bonds. So they try to seek a balance between the two, you know, some stocks and some bonds. And historically, in a balanced fund, the stocks are the ones that provided the growth potential—of course, stocks usually have a superior growth potential compared to securities such as bonds. Meanwhile, bonds historically have been looked at as safe venues and which give you income. And as I mentioned, a balanced fund in the year 2022 is better avoided.

An aside … the issues with bonds. The issues are right now that we have historic conditions, which do not favor the holding of long-term, fixed-interest bonds. The potential for losses is significant. Right now, the economy is over-indebted at the federal, state, corporate, and consumer levels as of late 2021. Additionally, interest rates are very low and if rates rise, that would be very hazardous for any fixed-interest bonds. Yet another factor that impinges on bonds is the fact that during the first half of 2021, inflation has reared its ugly head to a great extent because of the trillions being printed up during 2020 to 2021. Many do not realize that the root problem is monetary inflation (the excessive creation of money), which in turn triggers the symptom of price inflation, which is the inflation most are familiar with. But be that as it may, in such an environment, long-term, fixed-interest bonds (regardless of who the issuer is) are not a good consideration at all. Given the realities across the economic and financial landscape, keep your exposure to bonds and general debt to a minimum during 2022 to 2023. Given all these factors, balanced funds are not attractive at this time. So my favorite category of funds in the broad category of growth in income would be equity income funds, plus a side point is that studies have pretty much corroborated over many years that dividends tend to meet or exceed the rate of inflation. So I think that just gives an added advantage to the equity income mutual funds in this basic category.

Aggressive Income Mutual Funds

Let's go to the next three—the income funds. The first category is aggressive income. Now, when you think of an aggressive income fund, it might have a different name depending on who you speak to.

If you speak to folks that sell them, they're called "high-yield" bond funds. And if you talk to people who criticize them or are sceptics about them, they're referred to as junk bond funds. If you are seeking high interest, then an aggressive income fund isn't actually a bad selection if the economy and interest rates were stable. But in today's risky environment, the aggressive income bonds really have added risks involved. The bottom line is that aggressive income mutual funds will have lower-quality bonds that have a higher interest rate and are lower rated. So an important point to keep in mind is that if you're going to invest in any mutual fund that has bonds or you're investing in bonds directly, one of the most important things you should take a look at is the bond rating.

What is the bond rating? The bond rating is issued by an independent rating agency which reviews both the company and the bond being issued. They rate the bond based on the financial strength of the company and that it has the wherewithal to be able to pay back both the principal and the interest to the bondholders as stipulated in the bond agreement. The higher the bond rating, the stronger the company and therefore the safer the bond. The highest rating is AAA. The ratings of AAA, AA, and A are considered "investment grade." Once the ratings go to the Bs and Cs and lower, the risk rises significantly. The bond rating is a very important indicator for bond investors and it is usually included with the fund's recent snapshot of their portfolio. Of course, the lower the bond rating, the riskier the bond is as an investment. Lower-rated bonds do pay higher interest rates but this is to reward you for the added risk. Remember that sometimes in the world of investing, the issue is not a return *on* your money but a return *of* your money.

Given all that, if you are still determined to invest in lower-rated bonds because of their attractive, high interest rates then you might as well buy through a professionally managed, diversified aggressive income bond mutual fund. However, as a general point I would avoid this type of fund given today's (circa 2022) hazardous conditions that are especially true for low-quality bonds in this category. Next!

Conservative Bond Income Mutual Fund

For investors, this is the category to look into if reliable interest income from investment-grade bonds is what you seek. There are three primary subcategories here: corporate bonds, treasury bonds, and municipal bonds. Municipal bonds are in their own category and they'll be covered in the next section. Corporate bond funds (typically having investment-grade bonds) will give you the highest income in this category but treasury bonds (which may primarily have treasury bonds and/or treasury notes) are considered among the safest financial investments in the world due to the top-ranked creditworthiness of the United States. From a taxable income point of view, corporate bond interest is fully taxable at the federal and state/local levels while treasury is taxable on the federal level but tax-free at the state and local levels.

Regardless of which category you choose, conservative income mutual funds tend to play an important role in retirees' income portfolio. In terms of timing with both your personal timeframe and the economy in general, it is best to consider this category (real time) after our current economic conditions pass due to issues such as rising inflation, artificially low interest rates, and potentially rising interest rates. Once the economy is on a firmer footing and interest rates are higher but stable, then this category will serve you well.

Municipal Bond Mutual Funds

As I mentioned earlier, municipal bonds deserve their own category and this does have several subcategories. When you consider municipal bonds you are thinking tax-free income and this general category is for those that are generally in a higher combined tax bracket. A higher combined tax bracket means the total tax rate you are paying for federal, state, and local taxes. Your tax adviser should be consulted regarding your personal tax situation and how beneficial tax-free income would be to you. Say, for example, you are a high-income taxpayer that resides in a high-tax state such as California and you were deciding between a corporate bond yielding 3 percent and a California municipal bond paying you 1.5 percent. If your combined tax rate is at 60 percent, that means you would net more income from the municipal bond. Why? Because if the pretax corporate interest income dollar amount was, say, $3,000 and the municipal was $1,500, then how much would you net? The municipal would be triple tax-exempt so the gross amount and the net amount would be the same at $1,500. Meanwhile, the $3,000 taxable corporate bond interest income would be taxed at 60 percent or $1,800 (yikes!), meaning you net only $1,200. In this example, the municipal bond would be a better deal.

Keep in mind that although municipal bond interest income is generally free from federal taxes and states do not tax their own municipal bonds, states can tax each other's municipal bonds. This, in turn, stays true with municipal bond mutual funds. If you live in New York, for example, the interest from your New York municipal bond will likely be tax-free but if you live in New York and you have municipal bond interest income from another state (such as New Jersey or Ohio), then that interest may not be taxable in those states but will most likely be taxable in New York state. Again, check with your tax adviser for your personal situation.

Municipal bond subcategories. The three basic subcategories for you to choose from are:

- Aggressive municipal bond mutual fund. This offers higher-yield, tax-free municipal bond income through lower-rated bonds (bond ratings rated B or lower). This is the riskiest subcategory.
- Investment-grade municipal bond mutual fund. As the name states, this fund invests in quality municipal bonds that are rated AAA, AA, or A. These are most suitable for retirees that are in higher combined tax brackets.

- Municipal tax-free money market mutual fund. This would actually be a subcategory in the money market primary category but I include it here as well. This fund maintains a portfolio of short-term money market instruments and is suitable for those that are in high tax brackets and need to park their cash in a liquid, safe, and accessible fund until they reinvest the funds in another vehicle or use the month otherwise.

Sector Mutual Funds

Next, we're going to sector, international, and money market funds. The sector mutual fund category is another category I think is a good consideration. A sector fund is a mutual fund that will predominantly buy securities in a given sector such as energy, utilities, or consumer discretionary. A popular subcategory here is index funds which will invest in a portfolio of stocks that mirror a specific index such as the S&P 500 or Nasdaq composite. This category gives the corporate executive the ability to choose the (hopefully winning) sector and lets the fund's professional managers choose the individual securities inside the fund. Sector mutual funds (or indexes) are an excellent investing approach for busy executives. Monitoring the fund mix and rotating in and out of different sector funds as the economy makes its macro moves up and down keep the executive in control without needing to micro-manage any portfolio. A convenient way to do sector rotation is to make sure you use an investment firm that has a wide selection of funds (especially a menu of sector choices) so that switching in and out of any fund is as easy as a five-minute call or website visit.

International Mutual Funds

Who says that the U.S. financial markets are the only game in town? International mutual funds mean that you literally have a world of choices for your investment plans and being diversified geographically and geopolitically can have its advantages in terms of global diversification. Many investment pros like the idea of diversifying outside the U.S. economy. I am not a fan of buying individual international stocks (except for the occasional "American Depository Receipt" (ADR) security) but I think this is where a mutual fund has a real edge on your behalf. If I thought that investing in, for example, Japan was a good idea, then a safer and more assured way of doing that is to choose a mutual fund that specializes in Japan. There are fund managers that have decades of experience in that nation and this adds value to the phrase "professional money management" as a benefit of mutual funds. The main subcategories are:

- Country mutual funds. These funds specialize in a specific country. *So* if you are bullish on a particular country, the country mutual fund is a solid way to invest.
- Regional mutual funds. These funds specialize in a specific region of the world such as the Pacific Rim, Africa, or South America.
- Global mutual funds. These funds span the world looking for investment opportunities as they are not limited to a specific country or region.

Money Market Funds

The last category in our tour is the category of money market funds. Money market funds don't tend to be referred to as investment accounts, especially, since in recent decades, interest rates have been very low. They tend to usually be a safe place to "park your cash" until you either need the money or are researching new investment opportunities. In periods of rising and/or high interest rates, this fund does indeed become a good investment. The last time money market funds were a good investment was the late 1970s/early 1980s when interest rates were in the high teens (14 to 20 percent). This is the safest category for your money and the rates are competitive when compared with bank accounts.

There are three types of money market mutual funds:

- Regular money market funds. These invest in short-term money market instruments such as bank certificates of deposit, high-grade commercial paper, and other short-term debt in maturities of under one year and mostly maturing in six months or less. Very often the term is in days or weeks.

- Treasury money market funds. This type of fund usually invests the entire portfolio in treasury bills or other short-term treasury securities. If you want liquidity and are very concerned about financial safety, this is a top choice for your money.
- Municipal money market funds. These were covered in a prior section but included here for completeness. This type of money market fund invests in tax-free short-term municipal securities.

Unconventional Funds

I do not consider this in the sale realm as the earlier mutual fund categories but many executives want to consider more aggressive, speculative, or "high powered" for a portion of their funds. They can explore the world of unconventional funds that are really outside the scope of this book but they are worth a brief mention here. This category includes choices such as private equity funds, hedge funds, managed futures accounts, real estate investment funds, and funds that specialize in options speculation. Proceed with caution and confer with a trusted financial specialist.

Choosing an Individual Mutual Fund

In this segment, we'll talk about choosing an individual mutual fund. And I'll give you a multipoint approach to do this to make it very easy to choose a mutual fund that's appropriate for you and that meets your goals and needs.

Right category. Okay, first, make sure you choose a fund that's in the right category. Now, we have spoken in the prior section of this chapter about the various categories. And I think really that 80 percent of it is right there, if you can get to the right category. That's the most important thing because mostly people choose mutual funds that are just inappropriate for their category. You know, there's the 80-year-old retiree that has a growth fund, for example, or perhaps the 25-year-old, who's fresh out of college and ended up heading into their peak earning years but having their money in a too conservative fund such as a money market fund, for the most part. There're also people who try to get to growth oriented and speculative, when they should be more safety oriented given their particular situation. So the most important thing to keep in mind about choosing mutual fund is to please get to the right category. Now in terms of the right category, for corporate executives, during their working years, they should have a more growth-oriented approach, maybe choose a batch of mutual funds, where 80 percent or more are growth oriented. And make sure that it's adequately split between conservative and aggressive growth orientation. Right, then, when you're in your early years, they should be safer, more stable securities that are very income oriented, such as dividends and interest, and make sure that those are present in it. Because obviously, in your retirement years, you want more income, you want more stability, you need less volatility, and that would be more appropriate for you. So the first thing to keep in mind is the right category.

Fund longevity. The next consideration is how long has that mutual fund been around? If you boil down your search to two mutual funds, and they are both generally similar but you find out that one started just two years ago and the other one has been around for 40 years, that tells you a lot. All things being equal, I would choose the one that has been around a much longer time. I prefer a management team with a long-term track record where they've been through more economic cycles and conditions and experienced both up markets and down markets. I want to know that they've experienced much of the volatility and pains that have occurred over many years in the economy. Also keep in mind what would vitiate that point. If the mutual fund was around a few years but the fund family's investment management firm has been around since the Great Depression then that would affect my choice as well. The bottom line is that long-time, experienced investment management is a primary preference.

Size of mutual fund. The next consideration is how big is that mutual fund? In terms of portfolio valuation? Financial size is a real issue when it comes to mutual funds. If I was risk-adverse and I had to choose between a billion dollar fund and $100 million fund (again, all other things being equal), I would choose the larger fund that in this example is 10 times bigger than the smaller choice. Financial size means that the more money they have, the greater the diversification they have, obviously, a mutual fund that's diversified among 70 or 80. Issue is going to be again, all things being equal, a safer bet than one that has a much smaller pool of selections. The larger the fund, the more they have the ability to move money around not only among different issues, but also among different industries. And I think that's an important consideration.

Mutual fund fees. Next one is fund fees. The fund fees may not dictate how well the fund is being managed, but fund fees will erode gains for you over time. Again, if I had to choose between two similar mutual funds and the primary difference was one charged an annual fee of 5 percent and the other charged an annual fee of 1 percent, it may not be a material difference over a quarter or a single year, but it will be a significant financial difference over many years. Study after study showed that fees took a substantial bite out of your long-term financial success. Here are some of the fees to be aware of:

- Management fees. Virtually all funds charge an annual management fee to, of course, pay the managers of the fund. The rate will vary depending on the category. Money market funds, for example, tend to have low management fees. Aggressive growth funds, on the other hand, tend to charge higher annual management fees since this category requires more research and monitoring. Every category is different so make sure that you compare management fees of a fund in a given category with management fees of funds in the same category (so you compare "apples to apples" so to speak).
- Transaction fees. Find out if the fund charges fees for typical transactions such as exiting a fund or switching money from one fund to another.
- Sales loads. Many mutual funds charge a "load" or commission. This is basically a marketing expense when you get into the fund.
- 12b-1 fees. These are fees that are usually a modest amount (such as ¼ or ½ percent or up to 1 percent) annually for as long as you are in the fund. So if their 12b-1 fee is 1 percent and you are in that fund for 10 years, you will have paid

10 percent which, if you have a sizable amount in that fund, could amount to thousands of dollars … so ask about this.

- Back end load. This is basically a redemption charge. However, many funds phase this charge out over time so inquire about this one.

Mutual fund family/services. Is this mutual fund part of a fund family … and what is the suite of services for investors? All things being equal, I'd like to be in a mutual fund family since they may have 10, 20, or more mutual fund choices. How easy is it to switch between funds? Does the fund company have brokerage account services in case you want to be self-directed and purchase individual securities or ETFs? Also make sure they can offer various retirement accounts and services and are able to do total reinvestment and perhaps offer advisory services as needed. Now most mutual fund families do have these abilities, of course, but it's something to keep in mind that you ask about it, you know as you are making your selection.

Mutual fund performance. Last but not least, look at the fund's performance. I leave this one for last because the fund performance should "seal the deal" for you. It tells you how well they grow the account and how well they stack up against their peers. Now, I am of the opinion that you have heard from others that past performance is not necessarily an indicator of future performance. But to you the performance of the mutual fund, especially over an extended period of time, such as five years or longer, tells you that these people know what they're doing in terms of managing this portfolio of securities. I want to make sure that they are in the top 20 percent of their mutual fund category. In other words, if I was going to be looking at say equity income funds, I want to make sure I'm comparing apples to apples. How did this particular equity income mutual fund do versus the others in the equity income mutual fund category? Again, the fund does not have to be number one, but it would bother me if it was in the bottom 50 percent or the bottom 20 percent. Again, it's not an issue that it's going to happen again in the future. But it is an issue over how well did they manage it. Just make sure that the timeframe you're looking at is an extended period of time, no less than three years, preferably five years or longer. And make sure that they are consistently near or at the top of their individual category in terms of performance, and then you can move forward.

Managing Your Mutual Funds ... Points to Keep in Mind

Once you obtain a mutual fund or a batch of mutual funds that doesn't end there, you should be monitoring it to make sure that it's doing the progress you're seeking. For example, you have a mutual fund that's having mediocre performance over say the last three years. Meanwhile the market has been booming during that time that tells you that this is a problem with the management of that mutual fund and that it may be time to change to a different mutual fund company. View how well your mutual funds are doing monthly ... and annually see if you need to rebalance what you have. When the economy looks uncertain or worrisome, reduce your aggressive investing and move some funds to safer vehicles such as a consumer staples or utilities sector mutual fund. Keep informed and have regular conversations and portfolio assessments with your adviser.

Main Takeaway Points

- Corporate executives should focus on growth-oriented mutual funds during their working years.
- The focus should change to income-oriented funds such as equity income funds and conservative income funds as retirement age is reached.

Mutual Fund Resources

Investment Management Education Alliance (https://imealliance.com/)
MutualFunds.com (www.mutualfunds.com)
Investment Company Institute (www.ici.org/)

CHAPTER 6

Real Estate Investing Through REITs

Real estate investing is a specialized pursuit that requires plenty of time for research before you buy and plenty of time managing a property over an extended period of time once you acquire it. There are plenty of "how-to" books on being successful in real estate investing so I won't spend time and space in this book about directly buying, selling, and managing real estate property. However, I do want to cover real estate-related securities that I think are a good consideration for the busy, wealth-building executive.

In this chapter I will cover the most obvious and appropriate real estate investment for a brokerage portfolio, the real estate investment trust (REIT).

A REIT is a hybrid between a public company (stock investment) and a mutual fund. It is like a public company in that you can purchase stock shares through your stock brokerage account. Whether you buy 1, 50, 100 shares or more, you can make that purchase (or sell) easily with a few mouse clicks (or smartphone taps). The REIT is much like any other publicly traded stock investment: the underlying company has a management team, issues annual reports, and provides quarterly and annual financial statements easily found and viewed on major financial websites.

The REIT is much like a mutual fund in that instead of selling products and services it profits by buying, selling, and managing a portfolio of real estate-related assets. Where the typical mutual fund has a portfolio of stocks (common or preferred) and/or bonds (corporate, government, etc.), the REIT has a portfolio of real estate properties.

REIT Versus Direct Real Estate Investing

For a busy executive, direct real estate investing can be practically a second career or an active part-time pursuit. The more hands-on you are, of course, can mean more reward but successful real estate investing is very involved and management is an ongoing concern until the property is sold, very likely years in the future. Although there are rewards such as deductions (e.g., depreciation) and the potential for rental income and future capital gain potential, there are pitfalls and drawbacks. Because corporate executives tend to be at higher income levels (say, north of $100,000), tax losses from rental properties are either strictly limited or generally not tax deductible at all when reported as a personal activity (typically on Schedule E that accompanies Form 1040). Of course there are ways around it such as making the rental activity through an alternative venue such as incorporation or partnership (discuss this with your tax adviser beforehand).

Given the potential drawbacks, I prefer going the REIT route. Here are some important points to keep in mind.

REIT Benefits

Liquidity. Because REITs can be bought as easily as a stock in your stock brokerage account, it is more liquid than owning and managing real estate directly. Direct real estate ownership takes a relatively long time to buy and to sell. Even in a good market, it could take months until a successful closing date. Given that, I love the liquidity of REITs and the ease to get in and out if desired.

Income. Secondly, REITs are structured as trusts for their tax advantages. As long as the REIT distributes 90 percent or more of their income to shareholders, it can be free of federal income tax for the REIT. The great thing for you is that this means REITs tend to have high dividends.

Marginable. Thirdly, REITs are assets that you can borrow against inside your stock brokerage accounts. You can easily borrow up to 50 percent of the market value of your REITs and use those funds to buy other assets (such as stocks and/or bonds). Of course this is borrowing and should be done carefully since margin loans can backfire in a bad market.

Dividend reinvestment potential. Because REITs distribute their income to shareholders in the form of dividends, a great benefit for investors is that most dividend-paying REITs tend to have a dividend reinvestment plan (DRP). This means that you can choose the option of having your dividends reinvested into the shares of the REIT so that you can accumulate more shares.

This can be a great strategy for corporate executives that wouldn't need dividend income during their working years. Dividend reinvestment over a period of years means that when retirement time does come, you can have many shares giving you excellent dividend income when you actually need it. To find out if your REIT has a DRP, contact their shareholder service department or visit their site.

The Two REIT Primary Considerations

Just because a REIT is traded on a stock exchange, it doesn't mean that it necessarily moves in tandem with the stock market. A REIT's assets are real estate and real estate-related investments (such as mortgages) and their values generally rise and fall with the real estate market.

Therefore, to analyze a REIT, you do it it in the same way as if you were buying real estate directly.

Location, location, location. And you will also ask yourself, how about the location? Yes, you've always heard that real estate investing was about "location, location, location" and the same consideration is true with the properties in a REIT. For example, I remember years ago (circa 1980) a particular REIT had a large portion of their property portfolio in Texas. Oil's price had sky-rocketed during the late 1970s (inflation) but prospects for oil changed dramatically in the early 1980s as inflation ended which contributed to oil's sharp decline. As oil fell, so did the fortunes of the formerly booming Texas real estate market. The state's real estate market soon became a depression causing great pain for those investors and that REIT suffered huge losses which impacted their share price and also the income (especially for REIT investors). Yes ... location matters.

Fortunately in today's world you can find out about a REIT's holdings very easily since they are public companies and the information is disclosed at the company's website, their annual report, and also on many other major financial websites. Doing your research on REITs has never been easier.

What type of real estate? Does the REIT invest in office buildings or apartment buildings? How about raw land or nursing homes or cell towers? The type of real estate will matter given whatever the economic and market realities being faced at that time.

During 2020's global pandemic, some types of REITs were hit very hard, while other types flourished. Office building REITs were hit hard as the buildings were vacant due to lockdown measures and the general populace had to quarantine during much of that year. Some nursing home REITs were also hit hard as the pandemic took the lives of thousands of seniors. Meanwhile, as more business was being done online, REITs specializing in data centers and cell towers did very well.

The bottom line is that you must look "under the hood" of the REIT so you understand what type of real estate it is involved in and what good and bad results could occur given what economic events are about to occur.

Types of REITs

Equity REITs. Most REITs operate as equity REITs, providing investors access to diverse portfolios of income-producing assets they would otherwise not be likely to afford (or manage) on their own. These real estate companies own properties in a range of real estate sectors that are leased to tenants, such as office buildings, shopping centers, and apartment complexes. They may or may not hold mortgages but the bottom line is that the REIT directly owns and manages the property they hold.

Mortgage REITs (mREITs). The mREIT typically won't have direct ownership or management of real property; it finances through mortgages and other forms of lending. They earn money primarily from interest and also any gains of the sale of debt securities. Given that mortgage rates today (circa 2022) are generally low and the economy is experiencing both rising inflation and, on the horizon, possibly rising interest rates, mREITs will become more hazardous. For the time being, it is better to avoid mREITs and focus on equity REITs.

Hybrid REIT. As the name indicates, this type of REIT will have a mix of both mortgages and direct real estate ownership. If the mix is too titled toward mortgages and/or other fixed interest debt, then it is better to avoid this type of REIT for now for some of the same reasons mentioned in the previous section on mREITs.

Categories of REITs

Because REITs can be very diverse given the many categories of real estate, it is important to focus on the pros and cons of your chosen category and what its prospects are moving forward. In this section, I will briefly describe the main categories and offer the good, the bad, and ugly in terms of prospects for that category in 2021 and beyond if possible.

Office REITs. These REITs own and manage office buildings. In the wake of global pandemic, many corporations soon learned that many of their functions did not need to be in formal office suites and have downsized their office space needs accordingly. Prospects for growth in this category remain to be seen so it is better for investors to avoid this category until it is clearly back on a growth track which may not materialize until 2022–2023 or later.

Industrial REITs. These REITs own and manage industrial properties such as warehouses and distribution facilities. Until further notice, they face similar conditions as office REITs.

Retail REITs. These own and manage malls and shopping centers and related retail properties. They have been hit hard in recent years given the gains of online commerce but they were especially hit hard in 2020 due to lockdown conditions. Until the retail economy shows sustainable improvement, these REITs should be avoided.

Lodging/resorts REITs. Owners of hotels, motels, and vacation resorts and these REITs were hit very hard in 2020 for the same reason (lockdowns) as above. Fortunately, as the economy opens up and the pent-up demand for travel and recreation is allowed to operate again, these REITs may have a good chance of rebounding in 2022 (unless, of course, there is a repeat of pandemic and lockdown conditions).

Residential REITs. These REITs own and manage residential properties such as apartment buildings and other types of rental properties primarily for individuals and families. This is a more stable REIT category and should be considered.

Land resource REITs. These are REITs that own and manage properties such as timberland and farmland involved with growing trees or crops for the purpose of harvesting and selling to manufacturing and processing firms.

Health care REITs. These REITs own and operate a variety of medical facilities ranging from hospitals to clinics to senior and assisted living. Some of these REITs (such as assisted living) were hit tragically hard during the pandemic as Covid-19 took the lives of thousands of vulnerable elderly. However, as conditions normalize, these properties stand a good chance to rebound after pandemic conditions subside.

Self-storage REITs. Americans own a lot of stuff which means that REITs that specialize in public storage facilities for individuals and businesses should continue to do well.

Infrastructure REITs. These REITs own and manage real estate used for infrastructure projects such as cell towers and energy pipelines. This category should continue to do well.

Data centers REITs. Data center REITs own and manage facilities to store data usually for corporate and government clients. Because our economy is data-driven, these REITs should continue to perform well for investors.

Specialty REITs. These REITs may own and manage properties such as movie theaters, amusement parks, marinas, casinos, and other off-beat properties. Since this is a very diverse category, the investor would need to research vigorously for profitable opportunities.

Mortgage REITs. I have already covered this type of REIT earlier in the chapter but including it as an entry here to round out the basic categories.

Alternatives to REITs

I think that buying well-selected REITs is not a difficult task but some may prefer alternatives. Here they are:

Real estate ETFs. Why not buy an ETF that has the top 30 or 40 REITs that you can acquire with a single security … and a few clicks? A real estate ETF is a great way to gain the benefit of real estate investing coupled with diversification and convenience. For more details, head over to Chapter 4.

Real estate mutual funds. Having professionals actively manage a port-folio of REITs and other real estate-related securities can be a good way for busy executives to include real estate in their overall wealth-building plans. A real estate sector mutual fund can be a good choice. For more details on mutual funds, check out Chapter 5.

Real estate limited partnerships. Real estate limited partnerships can be a good compromise between the costs and risks of direct real estate invest-ing and the more passive vehicle of REITs. The main components of the limited partnership are the general management partner (GMP) and the limited partners ("LP"—investors such as you!). The GMP finds the real estate deal or project and structures it along with the financial pool from all the limited partners. All the partners share in the net income and capi-tal gains when the real estate property is sold. The best way to start investi-gating real estate limited partnerships is to check with your local real estate investing clubs through organizations such as the Nationwide Real Estate Investment Clubs (www.nationwiderealestateinvestmentclubs.com).

Real estate crowdfunding. Real estate crowdfunding programs use the power of the Internet to bring investors together with professional investors and investment firms to bring money together with promising projects. They have cosmetic and legal differences but they both operate with some similarities. In both programs, you as an investor pool your money with other investors and this is done in conjunction with professional investors and investment firms to create private real estate investment projects.

For more information, check out these websites:

- Realty Mogul (www.Realtymogul.com)
- Fund Rise (www.fundrise.com)
- Lending Club (www.lendingclub.com)
- Yield Street (www.yieldstreet.com)
- Peer Street (www.peerstreet.com)
- Crowd Street (www.crowdstreet.com)

Main Takeaway Points

- In terms of types of REITs, consider equity REITs.
- If you want great safety and diversification, consider REIT ETFs and/or real estate mutual funds.

- During economic downturns, recessions, or postpandemic conditions of 2022–2023, avoid cyclical REITs such as shopping centers, office buildings, and industrial development.
- For greater safety, consider defensive REITs such as residential apartments and cell tower REITs.
- REITs can provide excellent dividend income, making them suitable for retirement.

Resource

National Association of Real Estate Investment Trusts (NAREIT) (www.nareit.com)

CHAPTER 7

Alternative Investments

The bulk of the book covers mainstream investment vehicles and strategies but the proficient long-term investor need to expand the universe of choices to hone a successful approach during the economy's (and financial markets') ebbs and flows. Stocks and bonds are not always the best choice. Some off-beat investments should be considered in a properly diversified portfolio. How much of a presence? As a rule of thumb, these alternative vehicles should be no more than 5 percent. However, as your knowledge, experience, and comfort level grow, that percentage can increase.

Alternative assets do have the potential to do very well during adverse or anomalous market and economic conditions. During the late 1970s (and during late 2020/early 2021), gold, silver, and basic commodities outperformed stocks and bonds. Timber, for example, briefly soared by triple digits, which meant that timber-related stocks and ETFs soared. Although many would consider commodities an alternative investment, it is mainstream and there are many commodities-related stocks and ETFs worth looking into as inflation becomes prominent. In this chapter, I will focus on precious metals, cryptocurrencies, and cash (as in your bank investment).

Precious Metals

Whenever we discuss such things as precious metals the most common things that we are looking at are gold and silver. Gold and silver are precious metals that have a nearly 5,000-year history. These assets have retained their value over centuries when other means or stores of values such as cash or money or currencies have gone into the dustbin of history. As I write this in early 2021, keep in mind that we are just coming off from a pandemic and a lockdown and the government is now spending trillions which means that the currency supply will expand dramatically.

The problem is whenever you are in a period of economic difficulty and we are expanding the currency frequently, this turns into price inflation (the price of goods and services rises) and when price inflation occurs this is a deadly enemy to many investments such as fixed-interest bonds but the great thing is that in these kind of moments hard assets excel and that is why they should be a consideration for corporate executives in today's economic environment.

Precious Metals Versus Stocks (Performance)

Perhaps the best way to pique your interest in adding precious metals either directly or in related investments (such as gold/silver mining stocks and ETFs) in your portfolio is to illustrate the second major reason to own them (the first reason comes later), and that's how it stacks up against stocks and inflation over an extended timeframe—in this case, January 1, 2000, to December 31, 2020:

Vehicle	Spot price January 01, 2000	Spot price December 31, 2020	Gain %
Gold	282.05	1,887.60	569%
Silver	5.34	26.36	393%
Dow Jones (DJIA)	11,357	28,869	154%
S&P 500	1,455	3,258	124%
Nasdaq	4,131	12,870	212%
Inflation (CPI) during same time			51%

All the headlines were on the stock market, but precious metals out-performed both major stock indexes and the official inflation rate by a wide margin. Since precious metals do well during times of inflation, geo-political uncertainty and other negative political events, the prospects look bullish for precious metals during 2022–2023. But performance is actually not the primary reason to own some precious metals, so consider this.

The #1 Reason for Owning Physical Gold and Silver

There are several important reasons to have gold and silver as a portion of your overall portfolio but perhaps the most important reason of all is one that is rarely mentioned by financial advisers. That reason is *counterparty risk*. Keep in mind that virtually all investments and alternative assets have some type of risk. There is no perfect investment which is why the financial industry takes diversification so seriously. Proper diversification vitiates most types of risk (such as financial risk, purchasing power risk, and market risk). Routine diversification among conventional investment vehicles (such as stocks and bonds) removes most risk but the one risk present in all paper assets is counterparty risk and that is the one risk that alternative assets such as precious metals do not have. Understand counterparty risk and you will understand why hard assets such as physical gold and silver are valuable additions to any portfolio especially during times of extreme stress. Why? Gold and silver (and other, less prominent, hard assets) do not have counterparty risk in that their intrinsic value is not subject to the promise or performance of a third party. In their history of usage as a store of value and as a medium of exchange, gold and silver have never been worthless or "have gone bankrupt." During thousands of years of usage, gold and silver have outlived most currencies, stocks, and even governments. Given that, let's drill down on counterparty risk.

Stocks have company counterparty risk. When you buy stock, that stock is only as good as how well the underlying company is performing. If the underlying company is performing well then its stock will be strong and profitable in your portfolio. However, what happens if the company is not performing well or if market and industry conditions are adverse for this company? In 2007, for example, Bear Stearns was a triple-digit stock, but by mid-2008, the company faced bankruptcy and its stock went to zero. Enron was a market darling in early 2001 but it collapsed during the second half of 2001 and the stock was also eventually worthless. Countless public companies have seen their stock's value go to zero. Gold and silver have never been worthless, but companies' stock can go to zero (Chapter 3 will help you choose stocks).

Bonds = debtor counterparty. Perhaps the easiest vehicle to see the potential for counterparty risk is debt instruments (such as bonds). Bond investors ultimately seek the promised interest and the return of the principal. Bond defaults are not uncommon and in today's world and an unsustainable multi-trillion dollar bubble in bonds is a real threat to investors.

Currency = central bank counterparty. National currencies (also referred to as "fiat currencies") are typically issued and managed by that national government's central bank. If that central bank overproduces that currency (monetary inflation) then that typically leads to price inflation (rising prices). This condition of rising prices occurs when too many dollars (or yen or euros or whatever the nation's currency unit is) chases consumer goods and service. When this currency quantity rises and chases assets, for example, that particular asset rises in price and may cause bubblelike conditions that can be hazardous to unprepared investors. People forget that the famed market crash of 1929 (and many other market crashes) was preceded by asset inflation due to increased quantities of currency (and/or debt) and investors should be vigilant about those conditions (see resources in the Appendix for "early-warning" sites).

Currency collapses have been the most common collapses in human history and precious metals have outlived all of those failed currencies, and will very likely outlive today's currencies since political leaders and central bankers tend to eventually succumb to overproducing the currency they "manage." For 2021–2024, that phenomena is unfolding making the case for gold and silver (and other assets considered stores of value) strong.

How to Own Physical Gold and Silver

For beginners and intermediates, I strongly suggest physical bullion as a diversified holding in your portfolio and the easiest way is to get either gold eagle bullion coins or silver eagle bullion coins as issued by the U.S. Mint (see www.usmint.gov).

Bullion coins are the easiest way to add physical precious metals to your portfolio. Bullion coins are primarily priced for their metal content and a typically modest premium above the spot price. They are a better consideration for precious metals investors versus the second major category of physical metals investing, which is the world of numismatic coins (or collectible coins). Numismatic coins are a more complicated and involved transaction because there are varied factors in your decision. Numismatic coins are also about the grade of the coin, the date, the mintage, and the authenticity. The trickiest part is the coin's grade. The financial difference between one grade and the next grade could be thousands of dollars, and even coin experts could differ about what the true condition is of a given coin. Beginning investors are best advised to avoid that complexity and stick to bullion coins. Fortunately, established bullion coins (such as U.S. eagles, Canadian Maple Leaf coins, and South African Kruggerands) have a very active, global market where millions of coins are bought and sold every week. The U.S. mint has a listing of established dealers in bullion coins so it is not difficult to begin investing. Imagine buying some U.S. gold bullion eagles around the year 2000 when gold was under $300 per ounce; 20 years later that same gold coin could have been sold for over $2,000 per coin, a gain of well over 500 percent.

Gold- and Silver-Related Investments

Physical gold and silver are highly recommended, but are there more convenient ways to invest, especially through a brokerage or retirement account? Here are the major gold and silver vehicles that can be acquired as easily as stocks or funds:

Gold and silver mining stocks. In times of inflation and economic chaos, this industry does well. Their returns tend to outpace the price of the metals during bull markets. One stock I acquired during gold and silver's recent bull run (2000–2020) went from $3 per share to $47, a gain of over 1,467 percent.

Gold and Silver Resources

- Book: *Investing in Gold and Silver for Dummies* by Paul Mladjenovic (published by Wiley, 2020). A comprehensive guide on gold and silver for beginners.
- Precious Metals Investing blog site (www.preciousmetalsinvesting.com)
- The Morgan report (newsletter) by David Morgan (www.themorganreport.com)
- Top 25 gold and silver blogs (https://blog.feedspot.com/silver_blogs/)
- The Gold/Silver site by Mike Maloney (https://goldsilver.com/)

- Kitco (www.kitco.com), a top blog and news site by the metals dealer Kitco.
- Jay Taylor Media (www.jaytaylormedia.com) gold/silver blog with Jay Taylor

The world of hard assets and alternative investments could easily be its own book but in this chapter I will limit alternatives (after gold and silver) to cryptocurrencies and bank investments to keep this chapter simple.

Cryptocurrency

Cryptocurrencies (such as Bitcoin and Ethereum) went from obscurity (circa 2012) to the hot speculative vehicle to chase during 2019–2021. Cryptocurrencies are private, digital currencies that became popular in recent years as alternatives to mainstream currencies. They became currencies through innovative, new technologies (such as blockchain technology) that made these currencies very difficult to hack or to copy. In this way, they can maintain a strict quantity and have a quality necessary for valuable currencies—scarcity. Currencies that are overproduced subsequently lose their value (inflation!), a condition all too common throughout history. As cryptocurrencies gained notoriety and their usage as a store of value and as a means of exchange increased, they reached acceptance on the investing and speculative landscapes. It is important to highlight an important point: cryptocurrencies are a speculative vehicle and as such, interested parties should tread carefully. They can be very volatile so the safest way to participate is with relatively small amounts. Since cryptocurrencies have also gained acceptance as a means of exchange in business transactions (to buy/sell goods and services), this is the safest way to participate. More importantly, it is best to do your research before you make your first, initial purchase.

Cryptocurrency resources:

- Investopedia (www.Investopedia.com) is a popular financial site and if you do a search for "cryptocurrencies," you will find a tutorial and extensive information on what they are and how to buy/sell them.

- Coinbase (www.coinbase.com), a cryptocurrency exchange with extensive information, news, and views.
- Binance (www.binance.com), another cryptocurrency exchange with guidance for beginners and traders.
- Coin Gecko (www.coingecko.com), a blog with comprehensive information on the cryptocurrency market.
- A listing of the top cryptocurrency blogs and websites (https://blog.feedspot.com/cryptocurrency_blogs/).

Bank Investments

No ... bank investments (such as bank certificates of deposit and savings accounts) may not be considered an exotic, alternative asset but I include them here as a short-term consideration used for emergencies and contingencies when conventional investments are at risk. In the age of low interest rates (circa 2020–2022), it is hard to imagine that bank investments can play a major role in an executive's overall financial picture and they shouldn't. Bank investments play a different role.

Short-Term Needs

The main reason you should have money in a bank is for a safety cushion in the event that unexpected, adverse events may occur. What happens if you lose your job? Are you ready just in case you are temporarily or permanently laid off? If you have no bank savings to fall back on, then plan B would be to (prematurely) liquidate a portion of your investment portfolio. What happens if you have to go to the hospital because of a sudden illness or other condition and it might mean thousands of dollars in medical bills: do you really want to liquidate investments just to be able to pay this off? Now granted you should be having health insurance of course and you get it through your corporations as a corporate executive but you know how it goes: some expenses are not covered and there are those ubiquitous co-pays and deductibles. Have an emergency fund in an accessible account so your primary wealth-building plans are not temporarily derailed.

How much should you have in the bank for these possibilities? During good times when you are doing well, have at least 3 months' worth of gross living expenses. During uncertain or bad times, consider at least 6 months' worth. Some financial advisers are more comfortable with a year's worth. The bottom line is to have this emergency fund than not at all.

Bank resources

Bankrate (www.bankrate.com)
Nerd Wallet (www.nerdwallet.com)
Wise Bread (www.wisebread.com)
Federal Deposit Insurance Corporation (www.FDIC.gov)

Main Takeaway Points

- Hard assets (such as precious metals) are solid diversifications that go well with paper assets since they perform well (or preserve their value) during periods of economic upheaval, geopolitical conflicts, or rising inflation.
- Primary cryptocurrencies are limited in their quantity and can be a hedge against the unlimited creation of standard, government-issued fiat currencies (such as the dollar, the euro, and the yen).
- Having available cash (for emergencies, buying opportunities, etc.) is an important component and it augments your overall wealth-building pursuits.

Resources

See each individual section for resources in the above sections. For resources regarding the "big picture" of political, economic, and market macro events, check out the resources in the Appendix.

CHAPTER 8

Bonds

The Big Picture

In this chapter, we will be covering the world of bonds. And by and large, given today's economic realities and also the situation of the typical corporate executive, I can say typical bonds should really have a relatively modest presence in your portfolio, especially in your "earning years." But first let's just talk about bonds in general and later about what types of bonds you should consider given risks in today's economy and financial markets.

In the world of bonds, I can tell you what bonds are like, how they work, and so on. But that's fine if we're doing a textbook education. The greater value would be over the pros and cons, given today's economic realities.

First of all, a bond is an instrument of debt. When an executive, say, buys a $10,000 bond, that means to the corporate executive this bond (debt instrument) is an asset residing in their portfolio in their regular brokerage or retirement account. Meanwhile, that $10,000 is someone else's liability. In this specific transaction, the executive is the creditor, and the debtor (the organization issuing this debt) has to pay the creditor back the principal plus the interest on this particular liability over the indicated timeframe.

The most common bond categories are:

- *Corporate bonds.* These are typically issued by public companies (listed on stock market exchanges). They generally have the higher interest rates among these three categories but also entail the greater risk. Interest is fully taxable.
- *Municipal bonds.* These are bonds issued by governmental agencies ranging from towns and cities to counties and states. Municipal bonds are "in the middle" of the three categories in terms of risk. Municipal bonds' interest is generally free of

federal taxes. Additionally, states and localities generally do not tax their own municipal bonds but different states may tax each other's interest.

• *Treasury bonds.* These are issued by the federal government through the treasury department. Among the three general categories of bonds, this is considered the safest from a financial risk point of view. The interest is taxable at the federal level but tax-free at the state and local levels.

The bonds in all three categories are usually long term (up to 25 or 30 years) in maturity and the interest paid is typically fixed. If a bond paid, for example, 3 percent interest then that will be the interest amount for the life of the bond. A $10,000 bond maturing in 2040 and paying a stated nominal interest rate of 3 percent would pay $300 (usually in semiannual amounts of $150) every year for the life of the bond, and the bond-holder at the time of maturity would receive the full-face amount of $10,000.

The Bond Rating

Because risk and safety of principal is a primary consideration, bond investors should be very aware of the bond rating. The bond rating is where an independent agency analyzes the bond issued by that particular debtor on the basis of financial strength and the prospects of the principal and interest being paid as per the stipulations in the bond agreement. It boils down to whether this company or government agency has the financial wherewithal and credit worthiness now and in the foreseeable future, to pay the fill interest during the life of the bond and the principal on the date of maturity.

The bond rating is issued by independent bond rating agencies. The most prominent ones are Moody's, Fitch Ratings, and Stand and Poor's Global Ratings.

The highest quality (strongest) bond rating level is triple A (AAA) followed by AA and A. These levels are considered "investment grade" and are appropriate for conservative investors and those seeking reliable current income (such as retirees).

The levels go down to the Bs and Cs and lower. The lower you get, the more risk involved. Keep in mind that the rating directly affects the interest amount paid. The lower the rating, the higher the potential interest rates. There is a trade-off: you may get higher interest with lower-rated bonds but you will accordingly experience greater risk. And typically, you will be compensated for this greater risk with a greater return on your money or a greater interest rate for that particular security. So know full well that when you choose a triple A bond, corporate bond, and it's giving you 3 percent and then you have the lower-rated bonds (or in some cases, unrated bonds), giving you 8 percent, these are not equal securities in terms of quality. If you are concerned about quality, and the ultimate payment of the principal and interest, then of course you would go for the safer securities as evidenced by the bond rating. But if you don't mind taking on greater risk because you want greater income, then you may want to consider the lower-rated bonds but just understand what you're stepping into. The potential for a corporation going out of business by the sheer dint of its structure as a private organization in the marketplace has greater risk involved with it, because it's very rare that you see a municipality or the federal government, obviously, going out of business.

State and local governments and the federal government have the power of taxation. So they can have greater power to pay their liabilities or be able to back up their current and future debts through the mechanism of force, which is what taxation is all about. This in turn gives a greater level of safety. But, of course, that could also be abused.

There are many municipalities in the postpandemic period (circa 2021) that have seen their bond ratings decline due to the deterioration of their finances. Although taxation can be beneficial for municipal bond investors, the flip side is that if taxation becomes too burdensome, it will have a negative impact on municipal finance as taxpayers leave to go to more taxpayer-friendly jurisdictions.

In recent years, states such as California, New York, and Illinois have chased away individuals and businesses due to ever-increasing tax rates. This in turn meant less tax revenue coming in, which in turn meant lower bond ratings and subsequently greater risk for the investors of those specific securities. Meanwhile, low-tax states such as Texas, Florida, and Tennessee experienced a corresponding influx of new tax-paying individuals and businesses to their states which in turn strengthened their state's financial prospects.

Keep in mind that when you are buying a bond, typically what will happen is that if you bought a bond, then you will typically receive semi-annual interest payments. So years ago, in the halcyon days of the 1980s and 1990s when interest rates were significantly higher, a retiree could easily gain adequate retirement income from municipal bond interest as they used their broker or financial adviser to structure a portfolio of bonds (or bond funds). So even though they are semi-annual payments, you can structure it so that you can typically get interest every month; you might find you might buy one or more bonds, whose interest payment comes say January 01 and July 01 during the course of the year. But then you can buy other bonds, hopefully with the same level of safety and reliability, where they are semi-annual issues; payments may be February 1, August 1, and so on. So this is what happened years ago and those days could return in the near future.

But what about today's realities? In today's realities, what corporate executives need to understand and what all of us need to understand is that the current economic conditions about the financial markets and the economy have a direct and significant bearing on the desirability of having bonds in your portfolio. Because we live in a period now of economic instability in the postpandemic years and you have more debt than ever before in all the major categories, there's a significant quantity of debt out there, certainly in the trillions based on all the available data, but in addition, the interest rate environment is very low. And lastly, a great threat to bonds, again, is fixed-interest securities, which appear from inflation.

So, these three major conditions—excessive total debt, low interest rates, and the rising threat of inflation—make it very hazardous or at the very least a very dubious environment for owning long-term, fixed-interest debt securities, such as corporate, municipal, and treasury bonds. Inflation, for example, is an increasing concern. According to recent economic data in November 2021, the inflation rate surpassed 6 percent. And given that, when typical corporate bonds are earning in the neighborhood of 3 percent, now you're seeing purchasing power risk. Now, the danger is that what happens to all the bondholders out there who are holding 3 percent debt, but they realize that we're in a period where inflation is rising, and they are having diminished purchasing power with that particular bond they're holding. And then you have to also realize that in many cases, rising inflation tends to force, sooner or later, interest rates to rise. So rising inflation and rising interest rates will be a just a double body slam to the value of the bonds in your portfolio. In that event, many bondholders will choose to sell their bonds which, in turn, mean that bond prices will drop and investors may experience losses in their portfolio.

These are the unique risk conditions that we face with debt securities (bonds) during 2022 and beyond. Corporate executives (and retired ones) need to minimize their exposure to (fixed-interest) debt. For retirees, fixed-interest rate bonds that are locked in at lower interest levels will mean the loss of purchasing power as the rate of inflation exceeds whatever interest rate they are getting paid.

Granted, 5 or 10 or 15 years from now, the picture for debt securities may be significantly different than it is today. Also, your bond income strategies will most likely change. But in today's world, corporate executives who are still working should be avoiding bond (especially long-term, fixed-interest rate) securities and general debt securities by and large. But this is going to be an issue to analyze when the retirement years come along. And of course, during your retirement years, income securities, be they debt or stocks again, hopefully, are from a quality perspective that they will end up being a majority segment of your underlying asset portfolio because, at that point, we will be considering income. But now, let's say that you're a corporate executive today, and you are heading toward your remaining working years and you are hoping that within a year or two you want to start generating income as you either retire completely or possibly slow down your working pace (such as working part-time or working shorter days). Given everything I just wrote, don't dismiss the power of bonds. There are different types of bonds available and there are some that can be appropriate in rising interest or rising inflation scenarios. So read on for the details in the next segment.

Bond Strategies for the Corporate Executive

So after giving you a tour of the major aspects of the world of bonds, let's discuss some things that you should consider if you are going to make positive choices about adding bonds, again, debt securities to your portfolio. And let me just make three major points, which I think are going to be very important for your consideration. First, timing is everything when looking at the interest rate environment. If interest rates are high, perhaps high single-digit levels or possibly double digits (10 percent or higher), then buying fixed-interest bonds, such as treasury bonds or quality corporate bonds, is not a bad consideration because you're locking in a good income stream. Secondly, and as long as you remember everything else, you want to focus on quality and choose bonds with ratings no lower than BBB. Lower than that, bonds are considered more speculative and very low rated bonds are derisively referred to as "junk bonds." Thirdly, how you buy bonds matter as well—consider "laddering" your bond purchases. This means you don't buy 100 percent of your bonds in one fell swoop and lock in a single rate. It is better to stagger the purchase and buy some now and some later to lock in various rates and maturities which can limit your risk. Having some bonds at 8 percent and others at 9 percent can serve you well and provide some diversification.

But what happens if, like in the year 2022, you're talking about very low interest rates involved? Well, because of the conditions that could be hazardous—as I mentioned earlier, a low interest rate environment with the threat of inflation—long-term, fixed-interest rate bonds are really not a good consideration.

Adjustable Rate Considerations

Therefore, the best thing to consider if you are going to add bonds to your portfolio mix is to consider bonds that have an adjustable rate feature to them. They are certainly out there; just the way there are adjustable rate mortgages, there are adjustable rate investment bonds. And in this segment, I want to focus on at least two different types of bonds that are worth considering. They're both issued by the U.S. Treasury. So, from a point of view of financial strength, again, they're considered triple A and the highest reputation for quality in the world. But the bond that you want to consider to look at is the following. Number one, the "I bond."

Now the I bond is, of course, a type of savings bond. And you could be able to purchase these for as little as $25. And what happens is that the interest rate that you will get will be between a fixed-interest rate at the time of purchase, but also a component, and interest will rise during periods of rising inflation as measured by the consumer price index. So, this is a way for you to have an adjustable rate mortgage issued by a triple A source, namely the federal government. So the I bond is a strong choice—and the fact that you can buy in a given year, an amount equal to a minimum of $25. And I'm talking about the electronic version; there's also a paper version, but with the electronic version, you can make a purchase for as little as $25 at a minimum. And on top of that your maximum is 10,000 a year. In other words, the most you can bind given years is 10,000. All right. Now, that's the I bond. And keep in mind that the interest is subject to federal income tax; however, it's free from state and local taxes. And as an added feature, if you're buying it for the purpose of financing education, then it's possible at the time of purchase to see to it that this interest is tax-free as long as the interest is applied to the college tuition for yourself or a family member. All the treasury bonds mentioned in this section can be easily purchased through the Treasury Department's "Treasury Direct" website at www.treasurydirect.gov (Figure 8.1).

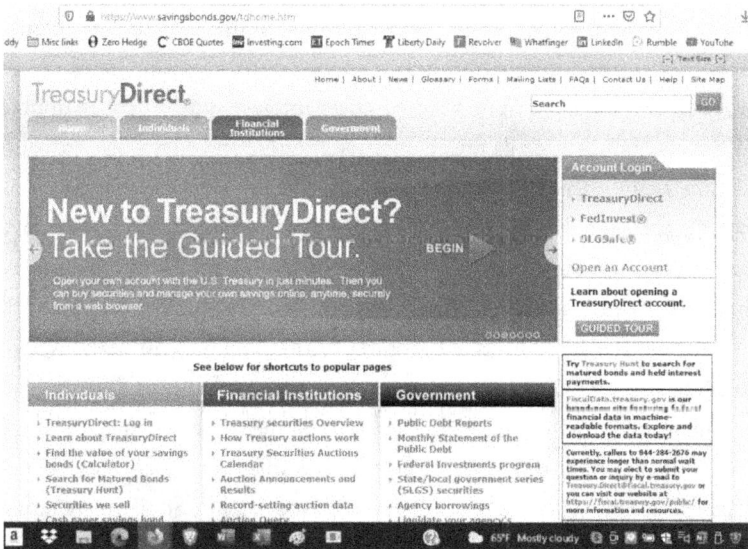

Figure 8.1 Home page for Treasurydirect.gov

The site has full details and opening a Treasury Direct account is free and easy. The great thing is that making the bond purchase at this site is easy and there is usually no transaction fee or commission. Your initial purchase can be as low at $100 with some securities the minimum can be lower (such as with savings bonds for as little as $25).

The second investment that you may want to consider is TIPS which stands for "Treasury inflation protection securities." TIPS can be bought for as little as $100. And the maximum is up to $5 million. So, you definitely have a range that is fine for most corporate executives. And when we talk about TIPs, they can be issued in terms of 5, 10, and 30 years. The great thing is that when they pay out the interest rate twice a year, it's a fixed interest rate. But part of the interest will move with the inflation rate. As inflation rises, so does the interest payment to the bond-holder. And if inflation falls (such as in a period of disinflation or deflation), then your interest rates will head down. In inflationary times TIPS can be a solid addition to your portfolio.

You can buy TIPS directly from the federal government at Treasury Direct but you can also purchase them through many banks and broker firms (details at treasurydirect.gov). I like the adjustable rate feature to TIPS coupled with the strength of the federal government behind them. This helps to offset both financial risk and inflation or "purchasing power" with the same investment. Keep in mind that the Treasury has other securities, which are fixed in their interest rates, such as double EE savings bonds (details found at www.savingsbonds.gov). You can also acquire Treasury bills, Treasury notes, and Treasury bonds, which have a fixed interest rate but they have different timeframes. Treasury bills have maturities of under a year so they can be a suitable spot for your cash for short-term timeframes. Treasury notes are intermediate term up to 20 years while Treasury bonds are long term, that is, 20 to 30 years. Again, you can start buying these securities starting with as little as $100.

Again, as I mentioned earlier in this chapter, when interest rates are much higher and you want to be able to lock in a rate, it becomes a beneficial feature in terms of the fixed-interest aspects of it. So if you're going to have bond securities in your portfolio, make sure again that they're issued by the strongest issuers and in this case the federal government is triple A; make sure that if you're going to be buying adjustable rate bonds with low interest rates, you don't have the risk of being locked in at low rates. You want to have an adjustable rate feature to make it safer, especially when interest rates start to rise. And the fixed-interest rates will be better in separate environments down the road.

Main Takeaway Points

- Long-term, fixed-interest bonds can be a bad place for your investment money during a period of low interest and the near-term threat of rising interest rates along with rising inflation.
- When interest rates are rising, it is better to be in adjustable rate securities.
- If you have long-term, fixed-interest bonds, consider selling to avoid potential losses.

Resources

To get full details on the world of bonds, here are some resources:

- Investopedia (www.investopedia.com) has great information and tutorials on what bonds are and how to buy/see them.
- Savings bonds information (www.savingsbonds.gov)
- Buying Treasury securities (bonds, notes, etc.) at Treasury Direct (www.treasurydirect.gov).
- Learn about the bond market at Bond Buyer (www.bondbuyer.com).

CHAPTER 9

Retirement Income

I start off this chapter with dividends because in a standard income port-folio (especially in a low-interest environment), the primary source of portfolio income comes from dividends. Whether you are talking about dividends directly (from dividend stock ownership) or indirectly (such as through mutual funds and ETFs), dividends are a prime consideration for the income-generation portfolio (especially for retirement purposes). I will wrap up the chapter with other income vehicles and strategies for the retiree.

Going From Growth to Income

The prior investment chapters focused on growth during your working years. This chapter serves as a walk-through of income strategies you can turn to once you make the switch from growth-related investments to income-related investments. The primary (and most basic) means of income are dividends and interest. I think that the most appropri-ate forms of interest income (given today's realities) are the treasury debt strategies covered in Chapter 8. For now, let's get to dividends.

Dividends

Dividends have the power to be a foundational part of your investment income and when you understand them you can benefit from them during the duration of your retirement years. Here are the principal reasons why a focus on dividends is crucial for the retiring corporate executive:

1. *Durability*. Chosen wisely, dividends can last virtually your entire life. There are companies in today's world that have paid dividends—consistently quarter after quarter—for over 50 years. Some have hit their 100th year.

2. *Beating inflation.* When you choose companies with a record of paying dividends, many companies have regularly increased their dividends year after year for decades. This type of income nicely complements those retirees on "fixed income."

3. *Predictability.* I find that predicting cash flow from dividends is much easier than figuring out where the company's stock will be six months or a year from now. This makes it easier to plan cash flow for retirement needs.

4. *Tax benefits.* The dividends paid by most companies and dividend ETFs and mutual funds tend to be classified as "qualified dividends," which means a lower tax rate (more on taxes in Chapter 10).

5. *Pay debt if needed.* If you needed to borrow money, say for an emergency or major purchase, you could certainly borrow the money in a variety of ways if you didn't have the cash at that moment. But unsecured debt (such as a personal loan or from a credit card) can have an expensive interest rate. Fortunately, your dividend-paying stock could come to the rescue. Say you needed $5,000 and you had a $10,000 portfolio of dividend-paying stock. You could actually borrow $5,000 from your stock broker using your stock portfolio as collateral (think margin loan). The dividends from the $10,000 worth of stock could easily offset the interest charged on the margin loan by the broker. Additionally, there typically are no monthly payments as there is with conventional, unsecured personal debt.

6. *Resilience.* Every now and then, the market has a correction or bear market event and stocks decline sharply. Moments like this can be unsettling and worrisome but think twice before panicking ... dividend stocks are resilient. First of all, quality stocks tend to bounce back after a pullback, even a scary one. As I have said before, good stocks zig-zag upward while bad stocks zig-zag downward. What gives dividend-paying stocks resilience is the dynamic between stock prices and the dividend yield. Say, for example, you have a $20 stock that is paying a $1 dividend. This equates to a 5 percent dividend yield. Presume that a brutal correction pushes that stock down to $10 per share—a wicked 50 percent decline. Should you panic? No. At that point, the company is still paying a $1 dividend (it's a quality

company based on the fundamentals which are covered in Chapter 3). With the stock price at $10 and still paying the $1 dividend, anyone buying the stock for $10 will be locking in a juicy 10 percent dividend yield ($1 dividend is 10 percent of the market price $10). At this point, "dividend yield hunters" swoop in on the stock and the stock price then makes a recovery. Sometimes that "dividend yield hunter" is you! If the company is fundamentally sound and profitable, then why wouldn't you take this as a buying opportunity and lock in that attractive yield?

7. *Compounding.* This benefit of dividends is more applicable to those seeking future income than current income so you'll see this covered in Chapter 3. This is the strategy of using a dividend stock's dividend reinvestment plan (DRP) to have the dividends reinvested in the company's stock to grow and accumulate your stock holdings over a period of years. This is a powerful strategy during the early years when you don't need the income. However, by the time you retire you have a large holding of the stock and then you will subsequently gain much bigger dividend payouts during your retirement years when you will need the income.

Dividend Payout Ratio

If you want to ensure having solid, secure dividend income now and during the remainder of your retirement years, then you should check the company's net income and the dividends being paid to make sure the dividends will continue to be reliable in the foreseeable future. A critical way to do this is to regularly check the dividend pay-out ratio (DPR). The DPR is basically taking the annual dividend of the company and juxtaposing it against the earnings of the company, and to make sure that there is enough net earnings to cover the dividend pay-out. The DPR is typically calculated on a "per share" basis.

Let's say, for example, you have a company that has $1 earnings per share (EPS). And let's say that their annual dividend is 60 cents per share. In that case, the DPR is 60 percent. In other words, the 60 cents dividend per share being paid out is 60 percent of the $1 EPS. These are numbers that are easily found at most well-known financial websites.

You can go to a financial website such as MarketWatch (www.market-watch.com) or Investing.com (www.investing.com) and enter the company's name or stock symbol in the search field and then see on the main profile page of the company both the annual dividend per share and the net EPS.

Ideally, the lower the DPR, the better. A 30 percent DPR certainly indicates a safer dividend than a DPR of, say, 80 percent. The highest you should tolerate for the DPR should be a maximum of 80 percent. That remaining 20 percent is like a buffer in the event that sales and profits temporarily decline due to a recession or slower economy. Keep in mind that real estate investing trusts (REITs) are a "different animal" and the DPR will not typically apply (more REIT income details later in this chapter and a greater coverage on REITs as an investment is in Chapter 6).

Dividend Income From ETFs

My favorite specific sources of dividends really are specialty ETFs that focus on dividend-paying companies. I like this for several reasons. First, the people who put the ETF together are the ones who did the analysis to choose the stocks that would populate the ETF portfolio. And for you, with a single transaction, you can get a whole portfolio of reliable dividend payers. Later in this segment, I will list several of my favorite ETFs that you should discuss with your financial adviser and see if they're appropriate for you now or in the future.

But as an example of why I like dividend-paying ETFs, one of the dividend ETFs that I chose was a dividend growth ETF and they chose companies who have had a record of 10 years or longer of consistently raising dividends. This dividend ETF could have been bought a few years ago for about $60 a share. And as of early 2021 the share price is at about $95 per share. The appreciation in the stock price was about 58 percent ... not bad. But the better news was the dividend growth. The quarterly dividend went from about 24 cents per share in 2011 to 92 cents per share in early 2021. The dividend payout increased by 260 percent ... nice!

So, given this, we often hear the lament from retirees about being on a fixed income. And given that, it would be great if they have multiple streams of income and that one of those streams of income is not fixed but actually grows at a pace equal to or greater than the rate of inflation. And this is the power that dividends from quality companies offer you.

Best sectors for income. Most of the prime dividend stocks come from sectors such as consumer staples, utilities, large-cap financial stocks, large-cap telecom companies, and real estate firms. In addition, you can use stock screening tools to find more dividend-paying stocks with sites such as Yahoo! Finance (finance.yahoo.com) and Investing.com (www.investing.com).

A sample list of dividend growth ETFs:

- iShares Core High Dividend ETF (HDV)
- Invesco High Yield Equity Dividend Achievers™ ETF (PEY)
- First Trust Morningstar Dividend Leaders Index Fund (FDL)

Please take this as information and do your due diligence before investing. Discuss dividend growth ETFs with your financial adviser.

Other Income Strategies

Interest income. Interest income comes from debt securities and the risks are real given today's economic conditions and prospects for investing in debt (such as bonds). For 2022–2023, investors interested in interest income should only focus on quality, investment-grade debt with adjustable interest rates. Find out more in Chapter 8.

Income mutual funds. Mutual funds that focus on dividend income are a good consideration. Find out more about mutual funds in Chapter 5.

Real estate income strategies. Income from real estate is great for retirement and my favorite choice is through REITs (covered in Chapter 6). Because REITs are required to disburse at least 90 percent (to maintain their tax-favored status as trusts), the income can yield 5 percent, 6 percent, or more. Keep in mind that the 90 percent disbursement is in line with these types of investment vehicles so no need to apply the DPR since that is more appropriate for regular public companies.

Noninvestment Income Strategies

Annuities. Annuities are insurance contracts where you invest with the insurance company a sum of money and they will make a stream of payments to you starting at a future date such as your retirement. Annuities can be a good diversification away from standard investments but you should discuss the pros and cons with your financial adviser. Too often, a better option can be a dividend ETF or an income mutual fund.

Writing call and/or put options for income. Call and put options are beyond the scope of this book but I do want to spur your interest on this topic as a discussion matter with your financial adviser.

Done right, option writing strategies such as "covered call option writing" and "selling put options" can be relatively low-risk ways to boost income in your stock and ETF portfolios. It is not difficult to boost income by an additional 5 percent or more which could mean the difference between just getting by during your retirement years and being truly comfortable. You can learn more about covered call option writing and/ or selling put options in the educational section of the Chicago Board Options Exchange site (www.cboe.com) and the Options Industry Council's educational site at www.OptionsEducation.org.

Main Takeaway Points

- A portfolio of dividend-paying stocks, ETFs, and mutual funds can be part of a strong foundation for income investors such as retirees.
- Finding stocks and ETFs that have a long-term, proven track record of dividends can be a good diversification from fixed income sources.

Resources

Resources to help you research dividends and other passive income strategies …

- Dividend.com (www.dividend.com)
- Divi Data (www.dividata.com) Dividend Hunter (www.dividendhunter.com) Cash Flow Power. This is the author's online course on investing for income. It contains dozens of investment strategies and resources to gain passive income (www.ravingcapitalist.com/home/cash-flow-power-i/)

CHAPTER 10

Taxes

As corporate executives work for themselves and their families, we have to remember to take care of our most expensive relative, Uncle Sam. Taxes are a daily reality and the more you can minimize them, the more you can maximize for you and your loved ones. In this chapter, I will focus on the two tax topics you should be aware of even if you are relying on tax advisers. Tax advisers aren't there every day to guide you so you should be aware of tax basics all year round so you can squeeze more value (and keep more of your money) when you do get tax guidance. The first topic is what taxes are potentially due from your investment activity and the second is tax-advantaged accounts to maximize going forward. Of course, you will discuss these topics with your tax adviser going forward.

Before I move forward, let's nail down the basic types of income you will come across and their category of federal taxability as well as cover them in subsequent sections:

Type of Income	Federal Tax Rate*
Wages and net business income	Ordinary tax rate (the highest federal taxable rate)
Short-term capital gains (less than 1 year)	Ordinary tax rate
Bank, corporate, or treasury interest income	Ordinary tax rate
Long-term capital gains (more than 1 year)	Long-term capital gains tax rate (reduced tax rate)
Short-term or long-term capital losses	Tax deductible but limited to a total of $3,000 per tax year** Carryover on losses beyond that level to future tax years
Qualified dividends	Long-term capital gains tax rate
Municipal bond interest	Tax-free

*Keep in mind that if the above types of income are inside a tax-advantage retirement account then taxes can be deferred or in some cases tax-free. (Tax-advantaged accounts are described later in this chapter and include accounts such as a 401k and IRAs.)

**The capital loss limit is $1,500 for those filing married filing separately.

Basics of Capital Gains Taxes

You may not be able to control capital gains taxes but you can certainly control when they occur: it can be on a short-term gain or a long-term gain. Your goal with stocks, ETFs, and other tradable securities is to hold the securities for at least a year and a day to qualify for the much lower long-term capital gains federal tax. Keep this strategy in mind—year after year—and you will save a huge amount in taxes.

When you buy 100 shares of a stock for $2,000, for example, and years have passed and these same shares are now worth $20,000, you have an unrealized gain of $18,000. But the moment you sell those 100 shares, that $18,000 gain becomes realized and then subject to taxes. But when this gain is realized makes a huge difference. In 2021, if that capital gain was realized in one year or less, it would be taxed as ordinary income and the rate could be as high as 37 percent. However, if that gain was over a year (by at least a day), the highest capital gains tax rate would be only 20 percent. This is one of the reasons that long-term investing can be more profitable than short-term trading and/speculating.

On your taxes, all your gains and all your losses are netted out against each other so let's net this out as well:

- If the net result (for that year) of all gains and losses is a short-term capital gain, then it is taxed as ordinary income at your highest tax bracket (as high as 37 percent for 2021).
- If the net result is a long-term capital gain, then it will be taxed at either 15 or 20 percent depending on your taxable income.
- If the net result is a capital loss of $3,000 or less (per year), you can fully deduct that loss against your other income. Just keep in mind that if you are married filing separately, the capital loss limit is $1,500 (per year).
- If the net result is a capital loss greater than $3,000, then you can only deduct $3,000 (married filing separately limit is $1,500). Any loss amount above $3,000 is to be carried forward to the following year.

For more details on gains and losses, check out IRS publication 550 (at www.irs.gov).

Reminder: Keep in mind that what I cover in this chapter includes capital gains and investment income that end up on your Form 1040 and *not* gains and income that are sheltered inside a tax-advantaged account (such as a 401k or IRA). Your tax adviser should understand the distinction.

Taxes on Investment Interest

Interest income from bank investments and corporate bond is fully taxable as ordinary income.

Treasury interest is fully taxable as ordinary income at the federal level but tax-free on the state and local (municipal) levels.

Municipal bond interest is free from federal taxes. Municipal bond interest is free from state and local taxation only if it is from the same state. Otherwise, states will tax each other's bond interest.

Dividend Income

Dividends are taxable but they fall into two categories: qualified and nonqualified. Qualified dividends typically come from common stock and they usually qualify for the lower long-term capital gains tax rate. Many funds that hold common stocks (such as stock ETFs and stock mutual funds) will tend to have qualified dividends that this category will, in turn, benefit the investor. Examples of nonqualified dividends (and therefore considered as the fully taxable ordinary income category) are dividends from REITs since the character of these dividends is tied to ordinary income such as rental income. If ever in doubt about qualified versus nonqualified dividends, check with the shareholder service department of the public company or fund involved (or check with your tax adviser).

The Power of Qualified Dividends

How much tax would you pay on, say, $100,000 in income? The honest answer is "it depends." I did taxes for 25 years and I can tell you that there are plenty of factors that can go even into a seemingly simple question such as that. But it is a good example to focus in since taxes make a huge difference whether you are a corporate executive or not. Remember the age-old slogan: "it's not what you make ... it's what you keep." Someone living on $80,000 per year tax-free can live a more comfortable life than someone living annually on a fully taxable $100,000. Let's use this example with three different scenarios.

Situation: You are 50 years old, single, and filing your 2019 federal income return (Form 1040). Your adjusted gross income (AGI) is $100,000. What are you taking home (net income)? I will leave out other factors and variables (such as state income tax) because I want to focus on the point that can guide you going forward:

	Character of Income	Assets Needed	Federal Income Tax is ...	Your Net Take-Home Pay
A.	$100,000 ordinary income (such as W-2 wages)	No assets needed ... just work!	$15,719	$84,281
B.	$100,000 in dividends (qualified dividends)	$2,857,143 (assuming 3.5% dividend yield)	$7,486	$92,514
C.	$100,000 in municipal bond tax-free interest	$8,000,000 (assuming 1.25% interest rate)	$0	$100,000

The table gives you some essentials for "your planning." The entire point of investing is to get you to a level of financial independence that works for you. The assumptions for both dividend yield and municipal bond interest rate are generally realistic and doable in today's financial marketplace. Your net income and your asset picture come sharply into focus. Given the realities circa 2022, the best goal for the corporate executive from the above three is choice B since accumulating $2.8 million in income-producing investment assets is certainly much more reachable than $8 million. The other reason that this is the more desirable goal is factors tied to today's realities of a low-interest environment coupled with inflationary considerations. Extensive studies done over decades show that dividends typically meet or exceed the inflation rate as reflected in the government's consumer price index (CPI). If five years pass going into your retirement years, general dividends will have likely risen. Meanwhile, the interest rate received from the municipal bonds, while tax-free, would lose value as the CPI rises past the nominal rate of 1.25 percent.

Given that, you would most likely need to sell some of the assets to meet cash needs for rising expenses.

Tax-Advantaged Accounts

When you are building long-term wealth, taxes are a major cost consideration. Given that, any reasonable strategy to help you minimize your tax costs and keep more of the fruits of your labor should be considered. The breakdown here will be in two basic categories; here is the first.

Tax-Deferred Accounts

A tax-deferred account means you can get the tax benefit in the beginning but later on the distributions are taxable. 401k plans and traditional IRAs are popular examples of this. Both lower your taxable income as deductions. The accounts can grow unfettered by taxes but as soon as you start to take money out, the distributions are taxed. The resources at the end of this chapter provide details on these accounts.

Tax-Exempt Accounts

Tax-exempt accounts don't offer a tax deduction when you open or contribute to them but the distributions are tax-free. A popular example of these accounts is the Roth IRA. These accounts don't provide a tax benefit but because the account can grow unfettered by taxes and later you can, at retirement age, take money out without paying taxes, making this a powerful choice for long-term investors.

A word of caution on these accounts for high-income earners: the tax benefit of these accounts may be greatly limited so speak with your tax adviser about the latest tax rules.

Final Points on Tax-Advantaged Accounts

The above, of course, is not a comprehensive listing and description of tax-advantaged accounts. There may be other accounts that could serve your personal situation even better than the basic accounts mentioned.

There are variations such as the Roth 401k and SARSEP plans, among others. If, for example, you are self-employed (such as having your own home business which I favor), you could qualify for the SEP-IRA which allows you to contribute up to 25 percent of your net business income every year with a maximum limit of $58,000 (as of tax year 2021). So, take the time to explore the possibilities and the pros and cons of all the tax plans available by consulting with a tax adviser experienced with the universe of choices in tax-advantaged accounts.

Main Takeaway Points

- Wage income, net business income, corporate and treasury interest income, and short-term capital gains are taxed as ordinary income (the highest tax rate category) if reported on Form 1040 (interest income and net capital gains may be shielded from taxation if it occurs inside a tax-advantaged account).
- Long-term capital gains and qualified dividends are in more favorable, lower-tax categories (as reported on 1040, unless they are in a tax-advantaged account).
- Maximize your contributions to tax-advantaged, retirement-related accounts during your working years to minimize current taxation and enhanced, long-term investment growth.
- Tax rules and regulations change or get adjusted regularly (typically annually) so get up-to-date information regularly from the IRS, active tax sites and blogs, and your tax adviser.
- Bottom line: tax planning is *crucial* for wealth building and achieving financial independence in your future retirement years.

IRS Resources

- IRS (www.irs.gov) for general questions, call their hotline 800-TAX-1040.
- For basic questions, consider the IRS's interactive tax assistant (ITA) at www.irs.gov/help/ita

- Get IRS publication 550: Investment Income and Expenses, including capital gains and losses.
- IRS retirement accounts information tax site: www.irs.gov/retirement-plans.
- Types of retirement accounts: www.irs.gov/retirement-plans/plan-sponsor/types-of-retirement-plans
- Traditional IRA info: www.irs.gov/retirement-plans/individual-retirement-arrangements-iras
- IRS publication 575: Pension and Annuity Income (how are distributions taxed?).
- For small business pension plans, get IRS publication 560.

Other Tax Resources

Tax Connections (www.taxconnections.com/taxblog/)

Tax mama (www.taxmama.com)

Turbo Taxes (https://turbotax.intuit.com/)

H&R Block (https://www.hrblock.com/)

TaxProf Blog (https://taxprof.typepad.com/)

National Taxpayers Union (www.ntu.org)

Tax Foundation (www.taxfoundation.org)

How to Make Any Expense Tax-Deductible. The Author's course on how to save on taxes especially with a home business (www.ravingcapitalist.com/home/how-to-make-any-expense-tax-deductible/)

Appendix

Ongoing "Big Picture" Resources

In each chapter I included resources that will help you further with the chapter's subject matter. In this appendix, I include resources that I find valuable to understand "the big picture" so that You can adjust Your portfolio accordingly to both minimize losses and maximize gains. There is no investment perfect in all economic and market conditions, but understanding which investments and strategies will excel in which market conditions will help you be a more successful investor over the long haul. Some are "mainstream" and some are "alternative," but all are useful. Check out these sites regularly:

- Zero Hedge (www.zerohedge.com)
- Bloomberg (www.bloomberg.com)
- Market Sanity (www.marketsanity.com)
- Gerald Celente's Trends Research Journal (www.trendsresearch .com)
- MarketWatch (www.marketwartch.com)
- John Rubino's Dollar Collapse blog (www.dollarcollapse.com)
- The Gold Silver blog (www.goldsilver.com)
- Financial Sense (www.financialsense.com)
- Seeking Alpha (www.seekingalpha.com)
- USA Watchdog (www.usawatchdog.com)
- Michael Snyder's Economic Collapse blog (www.theeconomic collapseblog.com)
- The Mises Institute (www.mises.org)
- US Debt Clock (www.usdebtclock.org/)
- Raving Capitalist (www.ravingcapitalist.com)—the author's site

About the Author

Paul Mladjenovic is an author, national speaker, consultant, and educator. He was a Certified Financial Planner practitioner for 36 years from June 1985 to March 2021. Since 1981, his specialties have been investing, financial planning, and home business issues. During those 40-plus years, he has helped hundreds of thousands of students, clients, and readers to learn how to build wealth through 2,500+ nationwide seminars, workshops, conferences, webinars, and coaching programs.

Since 2000, Paul has authored:

- Stock Investing for Dummies (all six editions)
- Investing in Gold and Silver for Dummies
- Currency Trading For Dummies (co-author on the 4th edition)
- Affiliate Marketing for Dummies (co-authored)
- Zero-Cost Marketing (all editions)
- Precious Metals Investing for Dummies
- Job Hunter's Encyclopedia
- Micro-Entrepreneurship for Dummies
- High-Level Investing for Dummies

He has done many popular live and online seminars such as "The $50 Wealth-Builder," "Ultra-Investing With Options" and the "Home Business Goldmine." The full details on his (downloadable) financial and business start-up seminars are found at www.RavingCapitalist.com (SEMINARs tab).

He has been interviewed or referenced by numerous media sources such as Comcast, CNN, MarketWatch, Bloomberg, Newsmax, Fox Business, Kitco.com, Futures Magazine, GoldSeek.com, Minyanville .com, and FinancialSense.com. Paul was born in a communist country (Yugoslavia). He came to the United States in 1963. This is why he refers to himself as a "Raving Capitalist." This background helps him understand the "big picture" so that he can provide better guidance and forecasts for his clients, students, and readers. He emphasizes a "two-pronged" approach to wealth building: "passive wealth building," which means having your money work for you (with investing/financial strategies); and "active wealth building" strategies such as starting your own home business or other active business part-time activity.

Index